THE STORM,
THE MOON,
AND
THE RAINBOW

SANDRA BARNHART

WESTBOW
PRESS®
A DIVISION OF THOMAS NELSON
& ZONDERVAN

WestBow Press books may be ordered through booksellers or by contacting:

WestBow Press
A Division of Thomas Nelson & Zondervan
1663 Liberty Drive
Bloomington, IN 47403
www.westbowpress.com
1 (866) 928-1240

ISBN: 978-1-9736-9178-5 (sc)
ISBN: 978-1-9736-9177-8 (hc)
ISBN: 978-1-9736-9179-2 (e)

Library of Congress Control Number: 2020908855

Print information available on the last page.

WestBow Press rev. date: 5/27/2020

This book is dedicated to my children, Jayson and Melissa, my daughter-in-law, D'Lynn, my son-in-law, Rob, and to my grandchildren, Emma, Jack, Drew, Walker, and Morgan. They have been and continue to be my inspiration, purpose, and meaning to life.

And to all my countless friends who have carried me through with their endless encouragement, faith, and prayers.

To Steve, my first love and mentor in life.

To Ron, who loves me unconditionally and helped me to love again.

And to my Lord and Savior, Jesus Christ, who has been my Best Friend, Confidant, and Protector all my life.

PREFACE

I began to pen my thoughts and post them often on my Facebook page when I knew this journey was going to end. It was a way to release my feelings, my roller-coaster emotions, the periods of hope and reality, and the periods of disbelief, despair, and emptiness. It is also about the healing, the changes, and the rising to a new path and a different journey. I wanted to express, and to give to my friends and others, my truthful and sometimes gut-wrenching testimony of what it was like for me to experience and to feel all that I did in the throes of losing someone I loved so deeply.

My aim, my hope, has been to convey to all that when their time may come for such that they will not feel alone, especially in their myriad of emotions, and that they will not be afraid to entertain any emotion, feeling, doubt, confusion, or anger known to the human race.

The book is divided into the following three parts:

1. "The Storm": This includes some history and events that happened as emotional and life-changing storm clouds gathered over a happy and loving couple and family in the grips of Agent Orange terminal cancer. It is some documentation of the ups and downs of the various treatments endured, emotional turmoil, and the continued living under the darkness, believing in the will and providence of our Lord Jesus Christ.

2. "The Moon": These were my thoughts, in prose and poetry, as the hurt, the loneliness, and the forever changes of losing a spouse of forty-nine years set in. It highlights a lasting bond between us: the moon, that lunar body that connected him and me forever.

3. "The Rainbow": It gives some insight into my thoughts and feelings as hope, the renewal of spirit, and the passion for living began to return to me. It is about my looking for new purpose and meaning as an individual, choosing what was best for me amid feelings of guilt and uncertainty. It speaks of journeying on a new path, finding new love, and new beginnings.

I have written these words with my honest emotions, prayerfully wanting to bare my soul, my heart, my rawest feelings so that you, the reader, will never feel alone in your own grief if you experience tragedy and loss in your life. I wanted to express that whatever or however one chooses to continue after loss is okay. Healing has so many methods of repair to a battered soul and spirit. It has various salves for different wounds. I have great compassion, sympathy, empathy, and love for you already. We may never meet in person, in this world, but our hearts will be connected and intertwined forever as you read my words.

THE STORM

I called them diamonds in the rough—the thoughts that snuck into my mind during my worst days. They were revelations. They were sunlight. They were gems. They were my salvation. Fragments of my soul that, for some ungodly reason, I chose to share. Maybe it was not my choice but a message for another, and I was just the means for the delivery.

All of life is about changes—some unwanted, some painful, and some a blessing. I am not here to understand it; I am here just to live it.

I was shopping for Christmas cards and relishing the beginning of my favorite season when he called. It was my husband, Steve, saying that, on what was *supposed* to be a routine scan to check his circulation, the doctor had found a nine-centimeter tumor in his left kidney.

You know the saying "It felt like I had been kicked in the gut"? Well, that is precisely the feeling I had at that moment. My heart began to sink. As a retired nurse, I knew that tumor was malignant. I was stunned. Storm clouds began to form. That was the beginning of the end.

I returned to work after that phone call, but I was in a fog. I kept thinking, *This, cannot be.* I had prayed for years and had asked the Lord with great faith, belief, and confidence to protect us, our little family, from fatal accidents and terminal illnesses.

We had dodged some bullets in the past. We had had a terrible rollover wreck in New Mexico while on vacation. Steve, our daughter, our son, their future spouses, and me. The rear axle had broken, and we flipped several times down the highway. The van landed on its side, and four of us did not have on our seatbelts. We were in the middle of nowhere, with Indian reservations on both sides. We had minor injuries, a cut elbow, bruised ribs, and two minor concussions, but we walked away. The state police who arrived at the scene told us we were extremely lucky. They had had a similar wreck the previous week with fatalities.

My daughter-in-law was diagnosed with breast cancer ten years ago. It was a small tumor. After consultation with the surgeon, she opted for a double mastectomy, and she only required minimal treatment afterward. She is now close to ten years cancer free.

We had a few more notable mishaps. Steve broke his leg falling out of the back of his pickup truck as he was unloading feed for his pigeons. It required extensive orthopedic surgery with the insertion of a titanium rod in his leg.

He also had a heart attack at the age of fifty-one while at a pigeon show in Oklahoma. My daughter and I had to hop on a plane during the middle of a terrible thunderstorm and rush to his side. He required a quintuple bypass to his heart, but as usual, he made a miraculous recovery.

I credited my prayers and trust in the Lord's promises for all the positive outcomes.

I always felt it was God's hedge of protection that I had faithfully prayed for—always. All these things that affected us, although scary and worrisome, were fixable. All this strengthened my faith, my belief that God was true to His Word. I believed because I had asked in Christ's name, and I believed my prayers were being honored. I felt peace. I felt protected. I felt God's hedge of protection all around us.

Steve served in the United States Army in Vietnam in 1967 and 1968. He was in the 101st Airborne, Fifth Battalion, Thirty-First Infantry, 197th Infantry Brigade 3 A. He celebrated his twenty-first birthday in the field while fighting the NVA and Vietcong. He was one of the smartest, most confident guys I have ever known. He was not careless in the jungles of Vietnam, so when an accident occurred in the field that required him to be airlifted back to the base camp—and eventually to the Philippines for surgery—we were all stunned, especially him. He was anxious to get back to his squad and to his good friend Sergeant Cohen. Steve had been a part of a three-man reconnaissance team that checked out the jungle ahead for the enemy and then would radio back for the entire squad to move forward. He received the Bronze Star for bravery, yet here he was a victim of an accident in the field.

Here is what might be the first fruits of my protection prayers for us. Ten days after Steve left his guys, his entire squad minus one was ambushed and killed. His beloved Sergeant Cohen, who had been due to return home to get married in a few weeks after two tours of duty in Vietnam, was shot in the head and killed by an enemy sniper.

I knew Steve's accident was God's work. It would not be Steve's time to die in 1968 in the jungles of Vietnam. Steve never saw it that way. PTSD and survivor's guilt or remorse set in, and it plagued him for the rest of his life.

Something else occurred in those jungles of Vietnam in 1967–68: Agent Orange. Steve said he remembered a wet, liquid mist coming from above several times in the field and covering him. It was intended to destroy foliage and reveal the enemy's whereabouts. We all know now it was not a good thing for the United States, boots-on-the-ground soldier fighting the war in Vietnam. In later years, Steve went to the local VA medical facility for his care and counseling. There he was encouraged to file for disability on his heart disease and his PTSD. Reluctantly, he did just that. After almost three years of constant paperwork and medical documentation, he was declared 100 percent disabled due to heart disease related to Agent Orange. Eventually his Agent Orange kidney cancer was added. I am confident also, that that was God's doing.

Before the plague of cancer hit us, we had a beautiful home on five and a half acres in a remote area in north Texas. He had been so happy for almost seventeen years, building a barn, pigeon lofts, gazebo, and storage houses—all the while traveling and working.

I had a neighbor, Barbara, who became my best friend out there. She kept me grounded and positive. I had been there for her when her husband was diagnosed with lung cancer and subsequently passed away very quickly. When we got our diagnosis, she became my spirit booster, my sounding board, my go-to person when I needed to release tension, sadness, or anger. I would cry, be angry, or just scream. She got it. No dearer, sweeter soul have I ever known. But there came a time when we knew it would be best to move into town, closer to the kids. We both knew there was a need to spend more time with our son and daughter and the grandchildren—for us and for them.

He made the move for me. I know his heart was low when he had to leave his beautiful haven, but that was him. He always put my needs, my happiness, first. The most loving partner, selfless. I do miss that, miss him.

So, we moved about midway through our battle. He never complained or was disgruntled.

He took it all in stride. As I look back on it all, my eyes brim with tears while thinking about how much he was at peace on that sweet little ranchette in Paradise, Texas. I try to look forward as much as possible today because to look back is just too painful. My belief is that he is indeed happy and at peace and well in a new paradise. I visualize him working on a beautiful place in the hills of heaven, building a family compound complete with ponds, homes, and barns. And, of course, pigeon lofts with perfect birds, especially Indian fantails—his favorite.

Even in sadness, my heart feels joy knowing this: that heaven, that paradise is what faith is all about. It is believing that Christ paved the way for me, purchased my ticket with His blood, His sacrifice, for eternity and a connection to the Father. An imperfect man and woman, Adam and Eve, messed it up for all of us in the beginning, but a perfect man, the very Son of God, restored and completed God's original plan. That is the essence of faith, the reward of faith. Believing that you will get to heaven—paradise, if you will—and to the Father via your one and only Savior, your lifeline, Jesus Christ.

When you pray for more faith, beware who hears that prayer besides our Lord. As a personal testimony, I can bear witness to the fact that the closer you want to get to the Lord, the more Satan will hurl at you, including the kitchen sink. Health issues, financial issues, job issues, people issues—any part of your life that the Lord will allow barbs. Just remember the Lord has overcome the world and all its obstacles, including Satan. So, hold on if you are in the fight of your life for survival in any form. I guarantee that He will not abandon you, but even better, God guarantees it. He is guiding your ship, no matter how rough the sea or how rocky the coastline. He knows the port to safely lead you to.

From the discovery of the tumor to the very end, although up and down at times, my faith in the Lord remained intact. I believed that God could and would spare and cure Steve.

We were first told after surgery that the left adrenal gland had to be removed along with the left kidney, but the tumor was encapsulated and completely removed, and the renal vein was tied off sufficiently. We were overjoyed with thankfulness to the Lord and to the surgeons.

Six months later, at his second follow-up x-rays, nodules showed up on his lungs. I knew that we now had fourth-stage renal cancer metastasized to the lungs. I was devastated, almost beyond consoling. I felt betrayed by the doctors and could not help feeling let down also by my Lord. Steve just wanted to get back to working and living.

He was always so positive and never, *ever* a worrier, especially about himself. He resumed life. Traveling, working every day, and coming home to take care of his pigeons, which was his therapy for his PTSD. I, on the other hand, could not get off the couch. I could not stop crying. I was beyond devastated; my life and my faith felt shattered. My every thought was consumed with disbelief. Praying every second, pleading before the Lord, uncontrolled tears, nauseating feelings, fears of uncertainty. I got all my prayer warrior friends across the US into action. They lifted us up in prayer, and although my heart was heavy, I began to float in their love and strength. I could not imagine my life, or the kids' and grandkids' lives, without him. My prayers were changing, intense most times. My world was drastically changing, and so was I. The storm clouds got darker all around me.

He was a remarkable person. He was reminding me, the one *not* stricken with cancer, to remember my roots, my God, my faith. He was one of a kind. He was amazing as a husband, father, grandfather, son, brother, uncle, and friend. Rare in this world.

It was about this time he also picked up the phrase "It is what it is." This was his answer to any, and all who offered sympathy or concern. He accepted it all: this cancer and its demons. He wanted no pity, and he never showed or expressed any anger or bitterness. He was never morose or down. He remained the most positive, happy, loving person throughout the next four grueling years of physical ups and downs and all the treatments. He knew and believed in who held his future, and he lived the remainder of his days floating in God's care. He was an example to us all. He never put anger or blame on his experiences in Vietnam that had led to this awful moment. "It is what it is." That is the line that has helped me to just live every day and to not dread tomorrow or fall into a deep, bottomless pit of depression. I realize life, all of life, comes under that heading. I think of it in some way every day. *It is what it is.*

He was most irritated about the fact that his chemo pills had turned his hair completely white. I thought he looked distinguished, even handsome. He was not vain, but he prided himself on his grooming and looking his best. I always saw him the way he saw me, with an eighteen-year-old's eyes. Just the way I saw him when we met in 1966, as he was coming up the escalator at Republic National Bank in downtown Dallas, Texas. I was fresh out of high school, taking my first real job at the bank in Big D, and trying to figure out where I wanted to go in life. He was a college guy home for the summer, working at the bank, wearing a suit and tie, and looking remarkably mature. So, the attraction began.

We had some new and different battles come up every month in that last year of treatment. He began to have hives and intense itching, a reaction to the chemo pill. He was put on prednisone at that point, and shortly thereafter, he manifested the effects of the steroid. His face got rounder, and he had some swelling of his hands, legs, and feet. This called for diuretics, more drugs. He had some issues with his kidney function, so we began seeing a nephrologist. It was a precarious balance between drinking a lot of water to clear out the kidneys and then monitoring his output to keep tabs on how the diuretics were doing their job. His pill box was increasing monthly, yet he continued to be active, work, and travel, enjoying life the best he could, never complaining.

We tried to keep things as normal as possible under the circumstances. I was trying to do that for him, and he was trying to do that for me. That is what you do when you love someone so much. We had doctors' appointments and CAT scans every three months. The target chemo pills were doing their job keeping down the small tumors on his lungs and not depleting him of too much energy yet. He was always upbeat and happy. Many times, I am sure it was for me he stayed that way, knowing how fearful I was of any change that might shorten our days together. He had a quick wit about him, and I know without a doubt that I laughed every single day he and I were together.

It was a bit more somber on our visits to the oncologist's office with the waiting room full. It was disheartening. We had such compassion for those other stricken souls who were just like him. We would whisper to each other that if Jesus would just come down and walk into that room, everyone there would be healed just by His presence. It was our thing, hoping for the Rapture. I am almost sure it was mostly my praying for deliverance from this dark pit we were in, because honestly, I did not know how I could ever exit without him.

There was a time in that last year and a half when I began to feel the crumbling of our world. The storm clouds were getting darker, and the winds of change were getting stronger. What my eyes saw was making my heartache so very painful. As a nurse, I had the drive to investigate renal cell carcinoma, any, and all studies, and treatments—conventional and unconventional. Although I knew it would take a miracle, I knew I had that kind of hope and faith. In my studies, I had come across some reports on the effectiveness of cannabis oil in treating cancer. Even with stage four, there had been some documented cures. I pursued finding it. I knew it was risky to buy it, and especially to have it sent from one state where it was legal to my state where it was not. But when you have love and compassion so deep for someone as I did for Steve, you throw off all fears and go with reckless abandon, no matter what might happen to you. You would be surprised at how many connections to obtain it there are out there, even among friends. I studied web page after web page. I was interested in any information on it and especially testimonials of people that it had cured. I began to get excited, and my hope was revived. I did find an interesting article that explored the thought that cannabis may have been one of the ingredients that God gave Moses in the wilderness during the forty years of exile by the Jews. It is believed by many to be part of the anointing oil detailed in the Old Testament. It is a plant created by God Himself. I have always believed that the cures for all of man's sicknesses can be found in nature, in plants.

I hope that anyone who is suffering from a terminal illness will never feel guilty or be made to feel guilty for trying anything that could cure them or just give them hope. Even if it is only temporary. Steve was reenergized with this new, natural, unconventional treatment. We both were.

With financial support from our son, Jayson, we continued the cannabis oil and, it gave us hope for about ten months. Then things changed very rapidly. He lost about seventy pounds. He had to quit his job, which he loved. His company, Reach, and his boss, Darren, had been so gracious, so exceedingly good to him. He had been allowed for a while to stay on the company insurance plan, and he was given areas of work close to our home. He could still be a part of the group and company that he truly did love. In every company he had ever worked as a salesman, he had always been in the company's top ten, most times the top five, and a couple of times the number one. He used to joke that all his high school teachers would be flabbergasted to find out he was making more money than most college graduates by doing precisely what he had gotten in trouble for at school: talking!

His perspective and sense of humor were always intact.

Around the spring of 2015, he started building Adirondack benches, using a pattern from a bench from the 1940s that we had inherited from his grandparents. He painted them either beautiful pastels or bright and bold. He sold some, but it was more about staying in life and being occupied with purpose. These benches would become beautiful, tangible pieces of himself that would mean so much to the recipients. His kids, his brother and sister-in-law, and one of his best friends from high school got one. Steve had contributed one, in his alma mater's colors, for his fiftieth high school reunion's auction.

So much happened physically to him at this time. He began to experience "chemo brain" and had lost his wallet and credit cards twice while at the hardware store. God kept me sane by answering my prayers of finding them intact each time. One time, I retraced Steve's steps from the store to home and found his wallet lying in the middle of one of the busiest cross streets in our area. Nothing was touched or missing. He had left it on his truck's toolbox while loading his wood and forgotten to retrieve it before driving off.

He was going down fast, but he managed to get up every day, get dressed, and be into the precious time he had left.

New nodules appeared on his ribs. Radiation and IV/chemo were then ordered. They told us it would probably be for six weeks and that there was a 40 percent chance that it would be contained for a while. We met with the doctor who was going to do the radiation, and he gave us some hope that these nodules could be destroyed. I held on to every ounce of hope, still believing that we could beat cancer.

His appetite had left him, and he was beginning to lose weight rapidly again, but on this day, after the radiologist's appointment, he wanted a hamburger. We dined on the patio of a Jack-In-The-Box across the street from TCU. It was a beautiful fall day. We talked a lot about heaven and how much we were looking forward to being there. Steve informed me, in his typical upbeat, lighthearted way, that he thought everyone will have at least a week of orientation when they pass through the pearly gates. I asked, "Whatever for?" He said flight training, and he was positive we will need it because he believed we would be able to fly. His humor kept me going, as did his incredible faith.

Some of the following writings are Facebook posts I made to let our family and friends know how Steve was doing. They were our prayer warriors and wanted updates regularly. No way I could have survived without their love and prayers and support. They will also show you a portion of ups and downs that we experienced due to the disease and the treatments.

For those of you who have known and prayed for us about the journey God has had us on for the last four years, I want to give you an update. Although there have been many ups and downs, I have always felt that the Lord was right there with us. For every down, although at times it was hard, we knew it was just an opportunity to trust him more, forgetting what we could literally see and to have faith in God and the unseen. Today at Steve's radiation consultation, I asked the doctor, "If radiation worked on the nodules on his spine, why wouldn't it work on those nodules on his lungs?" He said that it would with precision radiation, which I think is rather new. He reviewed his CAT scans and said he saw only two nodules that were close to his esophagus that could not be zapped, but all the rest of them could be. He verified to us again that all the nodules in his lungs had decreased. My prayer this week has been that the Lord would give us direction as to whether we should continue all the things we have been doing alternatively along with the conventional treatment, or are we just spinning our wheels and holding on to false hope? I think we got our answer today.

We are so thankful for your continued prayers. Every time, Steve's name goes upward to God in prayer it is for the glory of our Lord. We will continue the journey, and wherever God leads us, we know we have you all with us. I feel so blessed and honored to have so many friends who keep us lifted in love. I love you all so much.

Many mini miracles occurred yesterday. They really are not that mini to us. Amazing how sometimes as you reflect on a situation you can see that scenario the Bible tells you about. The one where we cannot see the unseen battles taking place between God's forces and the evil ones. Got a little peek at that. God reminds us that what was meant for harm, God can turn into good. Amazing how that works for you when you are His child and you have hundreds of friends praying for you. There is power in prayer.

Thanks to all our family and friends who have prayed tirelessly for Steve, me, and the kids. Although things are not as we had wanted for the moment, through your prayers, we have gained strength, courage, determination, and faith. I literally have seen God use a young physician, who we had never met, to come in and literally take over Steve's care in the hospital. In less than twenty-four hours, he ordered a brain scan, thoracic CAT scan, pelvic CAT scan, chest x-rays with every conceivable angle, and a GI consultation that has led to a scheduled endoscopy. He contacted our nephrologist, who sent his colleague to brief us on what his kidney function labs meant and the plan of treatment for that. This phenomenal young hospitalist has been in twice to give us updates on tests results. He has answered every question and genuinely displayed a care that I have never witnessed as a patient or a nurse. He has said that although Steve's diagnosis and new findings are not optimal, one could never rule out the possibility of a reversal of the disease or, in his own words, "a miracle from God."

Now we know that God is in control, and we know that He will either let us keep Steve a little longer with us or He may say that He needs Steve to come home. We are all okay with that. I must tell you that I believe God sent that specific doctor to do all the tests in one night. These should have been done before to ease our minds and to give us a clear picture of just what all we are fighting. I am just letting you know that your prayers are positively working. I have felt them, and I have seen them in action. No matter what the outcome, I marvel at our Lord's love and care for us as He charts our path and weaves the love, care, and prayers of friends and family into our lives. We want you to know that we pray for you all as well. We pray that whatever your cares, concerns, and needs are that our Lord will meet everyone in only the way He can and that you will be aware of how much we love you.

For all our prayer partners, I wanted to give you some proof of the power of your requests to God on our behalf. After Steve's endoscopy, it was determined that he had a stomach condition causing his nausea and vomiting and lack of appetite. Meds were started, and within twenty-four hours, he is eating small amounts with no problems. His desire to eat is returning. For the last month or two, he literally has only eaten one cup of applesauce a day and drunk water. He got the oncologist to write an order so that he can leave the floor and roam the hospital. The doctor told him there was one stipulation with the order. He had to promise to come back to his room. Our oncologist knows him all too well. Steve's strength is returning, and he feels like being active. His kidney function is returning to where it should be. His nurse and I determined that it was his pain meds yesterday that were making him talk kind of crazy. The doctor changed them, and that is better today. Our favorite hospitalist came in, and we encouraged each other. We exchanged our feelings of how God has intervened in Steve's case. We have had the care of six remarkable physicians this week. Although the cancer is not gone, and has spread to the bones, we are still confident in the Lord and His will in this journey. We have been blessed in other ways besides the physical needs. We have had so many concerns in our life at this time taken care of. Our children have been an absolute blessing. The remarkable owner of the company that Steve worked for never forgets the struggle Steve and I are waging. He sends caring messages that absolutely touch us deeply. We have had visits from our friends, our kids' friends, family, hospital staff, former coworkers—you name it. Your prayers have caused an avalanche of blessings, answers, and healing. We will continue the good fight with God and all of you, and with your concern and your prayers. We have nothing to fear.

First IV chemo treatment done. He also had another round of Aredia, a medication given to reduce any extra calcium circulating in his blood. Hopefully, we do not get into trouble again and then possibly stay another week in the hospital. He thinks the ribs are better today, so we are saying that the radiation is working. Chemo will be every week for quite a while. Providing he tolerates it. Side effects usually show up two to three weeks after the first dose. Please pray for none or at least minimal side effects. It has been a tumultuous day with a bunch of frustrations, disappointments, and annoyances. I take all of it as a way the destroyer tries to pick away at you when you are building your faith and you have so many people in prayerful agreement for you. First annoyance, my computer repair has turned into a blooming nightmare for a month now. Missy took care of that for me today, and she will pick up the computer tomorrow. The second thing was that I felt I had been ripped off for some health products I had ordered for Steve, but the owner contacted me tonight and apologized, saying the package was sent to the wrong address and returned to them. He is giving me a discount and resending the products today. Thirdly, today when we saw our favorite physician's assistant at the oncologist's office, the one who has been taking care of us for four years along with our favorite oncologist, he told us he was leaving in two weeks for a position at another facility. I was heartbroken and cried, right there in the office.

Then my iPad was the only one in the infusion room that would not connect to the internet. I had to observe all forty of the patients getting chemo for the next four hours. They all had anxious family members sitting with them, just like me. I prayed for every one of them. I hate cancer! It is no respecter of gender, race, or age. I know there is a cure out there. I just pray that God will bring it soon.

Lastly, to entice his appetite, I got Steve taco burgers for dinner, his favorite, but I decided I wanted Sonic. I was trying to be good, so I ordered a grilled chicken sandwich and a Diet Dr. Pepper with a triple shot of vanilla. That is my trademark fountain drink. When I opened the sack, I had been given a double meat hamburger with tater tots and a regular Coca Cola. You know what? I just said that must have been meant to be, and I ate all of it. Thanks for listening to me every day. Most of all, thank you, each one, for being here for us. I love you.

We are getting IV chemo today. You would not believe the amount of people here! This is just one small place in this big world. Multiply that around the globe. Why have the entities around the world not found a cure for these diseases, these robbers of life? Our fight continues. Another dose of radiation on the lower spine, probably next week, and an x-ray of the left femur that has been cranky. Steve's spirits are always up, remarkable human that he is. It is what it is. Take it as it comes. God is in control regardless. These are his mottos. I, on the other hand, had a rough morning. I had a pity party for a while, but I am better now. I am telling you all to go out there and enjoy health and happiness—and life. Drink life in. Soak life up. Be thankful for even the smallest blessings. God is good all the time. I read something today from Hal Lindsey. He said that as we approach the end of the age and probable Rapture, the most important thing we Christians will need is faith. I encourage everyone to really start exercising that immediately for any, and all situations in your life. Please continue to pray for us as we continue our assigned journey. Love you all.

Steve and Sandy at Texas Oncology today. Steve is getting hydrated for the next three days. He should have listened to me. I am pretty sure all will be okay. This is just a blip, but prayers are appreciated.

I am posting an update on Steve. His nausea and vomiting got out of control again, and on Friday, I had to take him to the ER again. I had exhausted my bag of nursing tricks, and I knew it had to be done, even though he objected. A great ER doctor decided that he should be admitted, and we are still here. I believe he is a little better today, and I hope that we can come home today. I am just not sure. Our oncologist feels that this nausea is the effect of Steve's fourteen radiation treatments and it will get better with a few weeks. I hate cancer! I know so many of you have had to deal with it personally or with a loved one, so you can sympathize or empathize. Mentally, physically, and sometimes spiritually, it wears you out. The cancer and the treatments are both devastating. I thank all of you for thinking about us and for your continued prayers. I am not sure what shape we would be in if we did not have you, sweet friends and family, behind us. Love you.

We are home! Constipation held us up for a little while, but those nurses have their ways to make one go. Tomorrow we go back to the oncologist for an update on our treatment plan. I have been doing a blanket prayer over all of you every day. I am hoping some specific needs are being met, but if you need more than that, message me. Please continue prayers for us. We are proof that God hears, answers, and works in many ways that only He can. Please pray for our doctors. I swear they are angels on assignment.

He had maintained close relationships with three friends from his high school: Max, Lynn, and Mike. Most times it was he who called and arranged a get-together, somewhere midpoint from where we all had landed. It was always the same "glory days" stories for forty-nine years. Yet when we were all together reminiscing and laughing, it seemed as if they had just happened and were being told for the very first time. He was a unifier, a loyal and loving friend. He was there for everyone, but he had a deep love for these three friends especially. On our last get-together with these three and their wives, he had begun to get nauseated off and on, having to excuse himself often to go throw up. Those three friends and those special moments kept him going. His love for life, his family, and his friends are why he wanted to endure whatever he had to—to continue the fight, to continue to live.

At one point toward the latter days, he had to receive several units of blood. I was sitting in the infusion room at the same hospital where our son, Jayson, was born. I could not help but be reflective, and my eyes welled up with tears. Such happy moments back then. Such devastatingly sad moments today. I clung to my Lord that day so as not to crumble. It is amazing what power God can infuse into you when it is absolutely, positively necessary to carry on under such a heavy weight. The term *Anchor* came into my mind. Yes, my Anchor was present that day; otherwise, I would have drowned in the seas of despair.

The days came for the worst, and although we expected it, we were not ready for it. We did not want to believe it. Eight weeks before he passed away, it was time for his fiftieth high school reunion. I was not sure we would be able to attend, but he was adamant that he was going. He had lost over one hundred pounds. He could not eat or drink without throwing up. He constantly apologized for his thinness and not being able to eat. My response was to put my arms around him, hold him, and whisper, "I love you, and I will take you any way I can have you."

Although he could not play in the reunion's golf tournament, he rode in the golf cart with his three friends. At the end of the game, he was awarded the prize for the "longest drive." Our daughter has a picture on her fridge. It shows him and me dancing our last dance together at the reunion. He was thin and frail looking, but I love it. It represents a very solid picture of true love, true commitment. Forty-nine years of the best, the worst, great joy, great pain, and a life bound up with hurts and healing, ups and downs. It was perfect with imperfections. It was real. We kept it that way. That is what you do when you really love someone. You honor the commitment. You dig in and let your roots with another find their way deep into the fertile ground of life and partnership. You will feel every emotion, hurt, pain, joy, sorrow, and excitement—just anything that touches each other. You truly become one.

And that is how grief is measured. As it is said, the greater the love, the deeper the void and grief.

The inevitable arrived and I was sickened to make this post, but we needed prayers, love, and friends at this time. So, I wrote the following words with feelings of total helplessness in the unreal moments I was living.

I have been hesitant to post about Steve lately, but so many people have asked. Therefore, I will give you an update. He decided three weeks ago to stop all chemo and alternative meds. He wanted to be able to spend his time with family and friends in a better way. I am absolutely inspired by him every day. For some, I know it is hard to accept a different road that you are put upon instead of the one that you had hoped and prayed for. Absolute unwavering faith in the Lord, no matter what, is the ultimate test for a Christian. There is no understanding for so many things here on earth, and I would advise you to never try to figure out the tragedies here. Build up your faith in Christ, and cling to Him. Our journey's path is a bit rocky at this moment, but we are proceeding one day at a time, knowing Who is beside us, behind us, and before us. We thank you all for your prayers and support, and we ask you to please continue with those for our family. For me, my "Facebook family" has been a blessing. It reaffirms what I already knew about you all. You are the kindest, most caring, loving individuals, and we are so very blessed to have you in our corner.

Most of the time, it was just sitting quietly by each other on the couch in the evenings. He would be working sudoku puzzles, and I would be playing video games on my computer. The TV was usually tuned to a nature or wilderness program. He managed to go twice to car shows, where his brother and sister-in-law had a food truck. He loved being with them; we both did. With them, we were always upbeat and always laughing. I tried not to dwell on the inevitable but love the day, embrace the day, the moment. I remember so well at one of the shows, only two months before he left us, he joined a van club. He had in the past fixed up a couple of vans and made them campers. Some of our best family moments were spent on the beach at Padre Island in Corpus Christi. It was the way he was constantly living, even though he was dying. I tell you now his spirit had supernatural power, and it radiated down on all of us. Every adjective of greatness you may apply to him. It made him very endearing to everyone on his journey. That is why our hearts bleed at the very thought of how he was and how we all were in a time when our world was intact, and we were all as we were before: happy and well.

We had a lot of visitors over that last month of his life. I am so grateful for each tender heart that came by to see him, to say, "I love you, you matter to me, and Godspeed." His best friend, Lynn, came more often than any other. He was so loyal so committed, and so connected to Steve. The gentlest of friends. His heart was tenderest when it came to remembering and thinking of their times together. The mishaps and adventures that the two of them had had or that the four brother/friends had had. To this day, four years later, Lynn still calls or texts me to be sure I am doing okay. The cream always rises. The bond of a true and loyal friend is never broken—not even in death.

The last couple of weeks of his life got very personal, and the reality of it all was overwhelming for me. He talked to me about what I should do about the house, the finances, the cars, and all that stuff that we had handled as a team. Then we had the talk. The one you just never think about until you must have it. Steve always put me first. He knew that at some point after he was gone, I would need to remember this talk.

He did not want anything left unsaid between us. He told me he wanted me to be happy. His words were "I don't want to go, but I have to go." He encouraged me to love life and live it to the fullest. He continued saying life is for the living and to be enjoyed because it is beautiful and good and a gift. It felt strange to hear him talk like this, about a time that he would no longer be here. You push a lot of things to the back of your mind when your beloved is facing death. There are just too many painful things to face and process. You must though. I am so grateful that I had such a loving, giving, unselfish husband for forty-nine years. It just was not long enough. Yet even if it had been ninety-nine years, it still would not have been enough time.

Our anniversary, on December 2, was approaching. My tears were many and often during this time. I spoke to him tenderly and said, "Please don't leave me on our anniversary." He smiled, kissed my forehead, and spoke with great confidence, assuring me he would not. He became weaker and weaker and reluctantly allowed me to call hospice. It just did not seem real. I was still pleading and asking God, "Why are You allowing this to happen? You could but look this way, and he would be healed. He would be a testimony to Your power and Your greatness in a world that needs to see it." It was not to be.

On the weekend before he died, the kids were there all day, not wanting to leave him. My mom was there, as were his brother, Pat, and his wife, Brenda. We gathered in the den around him in his hospice bed. He was in and out of sleeping, but when awake, he still had his sense of humor. Football was on the TV. The Patriots and the Eagles were playing. He raised his head and looked then asked Jayson, "Who's winning?" Jayson replied, "The Patriots." Steve closed his eyes, laid his head back down, and muttered just like a Dallas Cowboy fan, "I hate Tom Brady." Jayson grinned and said, "Daddy, you don't want those to be your last words, do you?" It cut some of the heavy sadness from the room for a moment. Later that day, Steve became a bit disoriented and began raising his arms up toward one corner of the ceiling above his bed. He had no strength, yet at this moment, he kept his arms up, reaching for that corner for several moments. He even raised himself up halfway out of the bed.

We were trying to get him settled and comfortable, but he wanted what was above him in that corner. I believe he saw his mother, father, grandparents, or maybe even Jesus letting him know not to be afraid and that it would not be long now.

Angels were in that room. All I know is that it was superhuman strength and a desire to reach what was above him in that ceiling corner. I still remember the feeling I had. Goosebumps and an awareness that angels from heaven were present in that room—and perhaps even our Savior. It was sad but beautiful and very comforting, if you are a believer.

> And if I go and prepare a place for you, I will come back and take you to be with me that you also may be where I am. (John 14:3 NIV)

His last day is kind of a blur to me. I knew when I woke up that his breathing was different. It was labored, not exactly Cheyne-Stokes respiration but getting close. It was Tuesday, December 8. I called the kids, and they both made their way to the house. We stayed as close to him as possible, touching him, loving him, holding his hand, stroking his cheeks. We whispered our love, our thank-yous, and our goodbyes into his ear.

I called the hospice company. Our nurse was too far away, tending to another soul departing this world. They knew I was a nurse, and they instructed me on how to administer these final medications. I will tell you it was not pleasant. Just before he passed away, tears rolled down his cheeks. Some will say it was just a physical thing because his body was struggling so hard to shut down. It struck me so differently though. I think he was hearing all that we were saying. All the love we were giving to him to take flight on to heaven. He was feeling all the sweet strokes we were gently administering to him. I think the tears were him saying, again, "I don't want to go, but I have to go. I will miss you so much." There was a powerful "I love you" in each of those tears. These are the memories, the forever thoughts, caught up in my heart and mind. Do not let anyone ever tell you that it will get easier, because some days it is worse. I will continue to live life and to love life as he did, as he wanted me to. Forevermore though, for me, the joy of life will be twisted together with the bitter sadness of losing a beautiful soul and partner—and magnificent love.

He was happiest in the country. That is no surprise. His spirit was untamed, but that is what made him magnificent in my eyes. The beauty and boldness of a life so freely lived makes remembrances both sweet and bitter to recall.

> All my soul follows you, love encircles you, and I live in being yours. (Robert Browning)

Strange, amazing, and complicated this mortal life is. With obstacle courses and fields of clover, weeks of pouring rain and many arid days, joy and sadness, strength and weakness, gain and loss. We are all walking the unknown all our lives.

My eyes cannot see you anymore, but I think of you always as you were. I can hear you so clearly, even though your voice is silenced now. I feel you with every beat of my heart but without the warmth of your touch. There are some things that remain so real, without explanation, long after they end.

I found myself in a place I never wanted to be, never thought I would be. I was alone. The good times and the love were over. When I was standing at the altar many years ago, I did not hear the words, and I did not entertain the thought. Yet here they were, the end of the promise. I had only heard the words "in health, for richer, for better." Now I was forced to hear the other part. I was there. It was the reality of a marriage and of life. "In sickness, for poorer … till death us do part." And now I had arrived at the destination I had ignored. I had not believed that it would exist for me. But the words were mine now. I was at that moment where I had been stripped of happiness, partnership, and marriage. I had to become someone else—someone I had no idea of or about or how to be. I was alone in every way imaginable.

I choose to remember him this way: a young and wild spirit full of life and fun. He never changed; although the body gave way, he remained the same. He was funny even in his last days. He showed me how to live, and he showed me how to face passing from this life to the next.

It has been four years since he was lifted from this world to the promised land. Not a day goes by that I do not remember something of us or think of him. Life must go on, but I can tell you from personal experience it is tough. For those of you who are yet to endure this, I must tell you that you will unravel *completely*. The threads of your life will be frayed and pretty much useless for a while. When God decides to knit you together again, you will be different. You will change, and that is okay. Life and death are mysteries. I try not to dwell too much on the negative or the unexplainable. Some things are just not in our control or understanding. The one thing that does remain, as the Bible tells us, is love. I thank God every day for that. For His love, Steve's love, my kids' love, my friends' love, my mother's love, and for new love. That is the one sweet salve that heals every hurt there is. We must all find our own way through these things. My journey will not be your journey, but I want you to know that my heart will understand your heart and love you. Even if it is from afar until you are mended back together.

Steve taught me many things. The main thing he taught me was what real love is. I am making my way along a new path. I hope I am making him proud.

THE MOON

I make my way by the moonlight now, and not just at night but always. It is ever-present in my heart, mind, and soul. I watched him one evening in his lawn chair outside, bathed in the glow of a super moon. He spoke gently of the Creator and of His creations as if in a trance. He was in a different realm from where I was sitting, although we were only inches apart. I knew at that moment that he was letting go. He was already between heaven and earth, being led by the Power that dispersed that light from above. I can never forget that night, that light, that moment. Now I am joined to the moon and its glow forever. It was the last thing we shared together. The last thing we loved together. So, I feel he comes to me now, in the moonlight, and when I look upon it, I sense his strength, his presence, and his love.

No one understood but her and him. She was here. He was way past the moon now, but he spoke to her and he led her every day. No one understood but her and him. She knew what he was doing and that it is why it all felt so good, so right. That is why the tears rained down her cheeks some nights. It was not sadness but gratitude and love. She knew his love for her was eternal. He spoke to her. He led her every day. Her happiness was still the most important thing to him, her lover who was way past the moon now, and no one understood but her and him.

You know how the sun can be shining yet it is raining at the same time? That is how I describe me most days now. That is the perfect description of a widow. I know that in nature when this sun and rain thing occurs, a rainbow appears eventually. I am sure it will occur sometime in widow-life. It may be in a new purpose or in a new passion. I don't want to hear, "You just need to be patient" or "All in God's time." Those thoughts come from people who are not widows or widowers. Someday those will understand and remember those words. Adjustments are difficult to make, but the spirit continues to hope. And so together the rain falls and the sun shines until things are right again.

For the good things, the right things, the things of quality, the sweet things, the true things, and the real thing, be patient, be prayerful, and always be hopeful.

Happiness is writing pretty words for others in the moonlight, connecting with a special person, or sleeping on a pallet of quilts piled high with your grandbabies. It is going out to dinner with your kids, taking your mom for ice cream, or hearing from your friends and making plans to spend time with them. And sometimes Facebook on Saturday night until something else comes along.

And the moon said, "Always make the most of your opportunities to shine. For it may be by your light that another will find their way."

In the stillness of the night, she found solace compared to no other. There she could be lost in thoughts uninterrupted. She could see the past vividly and hear the voices of those long gone. Memories, like priceless jewels, held in the vault of her heart and etched in her mind. And as the moon rose every evening, its glow led her to her solace. It was a paradox of hurt and healing.

Somewhere in the moonlight, far away from the city lights, there is a place you can park your pickup truck, put the quilt in the bed, lie back, and just look up into the heavens. Memories, hopes, and dreams will collide. You can talk to God, or you can just be silent and let the sights permeate your mind. There is much to be said about peace and quiet, but oh so much more when it is under the light of the moon and the stars in the big Texas sky.

Something stirs in the heart at the sight of a full moon. Dreams are formed. Love is born. Memories of life unfold like a movie reel. I live for the magic of a full moon. Bewitched am I by moonlight, bathed in its glow with feelings of happiness, hopefulness, and wonder.

The moon never disappoints her. She sees something different every night that it makes an appearance. Beautiful things happen in the moonlight. Remembrances dear and deep are conjured up in the moonbeams. Sweet life is magnified in its golden glow. All the world is hushed to her as she gazes upon the one constant that will forever bring her joy and a connection to heaven. She longs to see beyond its brightness into a promised paradise of endless happiness and perfection. But for now, she will relish and love to the utmost the lunar beauty and mystique that the heavens choose to display on this earthly side.

If I climb up to the moon, I know he will be there, and we will talk of all the love we had and all the love yet to come. He will tell me of wondrous things he has seen and heard, and I will tell him I miss him so.

I dreamed that I was up above the earth, my feet upon the clouds. And when I looked down, I saw everyone I had ever loved, including those who had passed and those still upon the land. My heart was happy, and my eyes filled with tears because we were as we were before. And as I drifted above loving them, I felt a warmness of what I surely thought was the sun's light above me. But it was a different warmth. It was satisfying, encompassing warmth, and I realized it was coming from my heart. If I had never awakened from this beautiful dream, my longings would have been fulfilled.

No matter where the full moon glows, it paints a masterpiece down below. God's artwork fills the sky, a preview of our glory by and by.

Yes, I did not realize that the days would become filled with many more hours than they used to have when he was here. And although I have found so many new friends, the joy is not as joyful. When you must change, due to a death of someone you loved intensely, be it a spouse or a child, friend, or family member, your evolution is painful. You keep telling yourself that the ache in your chest and the pain in your gut will ease someday. But the mind, with its memories, feeds the pain to your breaking point at times. You look through the tears and wonder how in the world you still exist. But here you are, still standing, a little bent and a tad unsteady. Life speeds by, but instead of wanting it to slow down, you now cheer for it to zoom ahead at record speed. Just know that there is no preparation for loss—great loss. You can play it over and over in your mind how you think things will be, but trust me: the script is unwritten, and the scene is not known until it occurs. When it occurs for you, then and only then will you understand what I feel at this very moment.

While the days are passing by, there is so much going on all around us. Some things we choose to know about and some we choose not to entertain a thought toward. Then sometimes you get directed to know and think about things way beyond yourself and your own little world. I have had changes that I did not want but were made by a Supreme will that is far more intelligent in making decisions with motives and meanings than I will ever understand. I was asked to join a private group on Facebook for widows and widowers. At first, I was apprehensive because sharing my deepest personal feelings with strangers has not always been the way I am. But as I began to read posts from so many, I was moved and enlightened. These were from grieving people from across the world. Some were young with small children or babies on the way. The causes for their widowed state varied from disease to accidents to sheer tragedies. Each story I read was like ripples on top of water after a pebble is thrown. I read of the far-reaching effects these deaths had had, not only on the wife or husband but also on the children, the siblings, the parents, the friends, and sometimes the communities. It is staggering how much loss of life there is twenty-four hours a day, seven days a week. Lives, dreams, futures, and plans changed forever. I feel so fortunate in my grief and heartache because I had my love with me for a long time.

It is strange but wonderful how God works. I was turned off at first by the posts, but when I started to respond to some of them, I felt an instant closeness, belonging, and usefulness. We were all in individual stages of grieving. Some were angry or bitter. Some were just numb. Some were still struggling with extreme sadness even after many years. I saw great compassion and understanding from most for others needing a tender word of understanding. It is a community, a shelter to retreat to, to vent, to praise, to ask for prayers, or to share a sign from a loved one. It is also a place to express some humor or share a favorite song. It is a city where everyone shares the same things: a broken heart, loss, shattered dreams, fear, doubts, uncertainty, and loneliness. Yet in each other, we found some understanding, love, and hope. I tell you things just to remind you to love each other, be kind to each other, and enjoy your time here. Just realize that there are serious, life-changing things occurring around you every minute of the day. Choose your words wisely, and everything you do, do it with passion and compassion.

Never am I alone in the moonlight, for the peace of the misty glow on black skies keeps my mind transfixed on whose I am. The keeper of His promises, the Eternal El Olam, the Everlasting God surrounds me with His love.

It is no secret that I love the moon. On nights like this when it is so incredibly beautiful, I remember why I love it and what it means to me in a personal way. I think the hardest things in life are the devastating changes you did not ask for. The ones that occur at a time in your life when you do not want to be through living. Perhaps the most awful feeling in the world is to lose the one who meant the world to you, and vice versa. I miss meaning the world to someone. I miss getting the compliments from that someone who really means it. I miss that look between my other half and me that only we understand. I miss everything about a bonded loving relationship. I am not sure anyone—friends, family, kids, or the world at large—will get it unless they are there or have been there. As I move forward, I take my direction from the Lord. He has protected me and led me all my life. I have been the prodigal at times but have always found my way back. He is leading me forward. I am happy. Some things will never change. The goodness of my past life is a big part of why I can move forward. I have new things in my life—good things. They make me happy. I am pursuing them because when I talk to God, He gives me no reason to doubt myself. What I feel is His love, and He reminds me of my husband's tender words to me when he was leaving this world. "Life is for the living and enjoying. Live it like you want and need to. It is way too short. Enjoy it while you can." That is what I am going to do.

Memories are so painful, yet I stroke them like a bruise upon my soul. There is no healing. There is no relief. There is only pretense and a mask of feelings that become more permanent every moment. If truth be told by all who have lost a love so dear, the honesty would be drowned in tears and the spirit would be battered forevermore.

You know the saddest thing about loving someone for forty-nine years and losing them? It is that you are really no one's priority anymore. It takes some time to become accustomed to it. It is not that you need attention from anyone. On the contrary, it is just that the one who held you in the highest esteem with love, gratitude, and importance is no longer there. That is the essence of the widow's loneliness.

My thought and truth for today: After you lose someone you love, no one can fix you. No one can put the broken pieces of your life back together and make you whole or the same again. Because the pieces that are broken do not fit together anymore to make you who you used to be. There are many things that change, but the one that is most difficult, the biggest challenge, the highest hurdle, is transforming yourself into someone different from who you have been for so long. Your core may stay intact, but every thought, every action, and daily living are done with a totally new mind, a totally different way. The people you know look at you differently, think of you differently, respond to you differently, and talk to you differently. Adjustments are up to you. Choices are up to you. Changes are up to you. My advice to myself is found in lines from the western movie *Tombstone*. I mix them up from time to time, depending on what I need to hear from myself. Basically, it is this: Life is what it is. There is no normal life. It is just life, and you must get on with it regardless.

> For God has not given us a spirit of timidity, but a spirit of power, of love and of a self-discipline. (2 Timothy 1:7 NIV)

I posted this on Facebook when we were in the end stages of cancer. I held on to this verse and many others. I had a bold spirit then. I did not hesitate to ask for things or to be angry with God when things looked bleak. It was confusing, troubling, and depressing to believe so strongly yet not get the answer I so firmly believed God would grant. I came out of all this pretty weak and stripped of understanding. I learned all about faith, my faith. It really has more to do with when we do not get the answer we want.

It has been almost four years. My, my, how I have learned so much about myself, and so very much about others. There is a constant battle within me. I am literally two people: the before and the after. No one, not even all the saints of all the ages, could come through the pits of life and not be changed. I have learned to wear my armor and to keep my thoughts on my path. I realize that God may not spare you from burdens or pain or loss, but He and He alone is your personal guide, your physician, your counselor, your sounding board, and even at times, your punching bag. I am so eternally grateful for my relationship with Him, and that, my friends, is exactly how all the saints of all the ages have come through the pits of life, watching the light of the Lord up ahead leading all the way.

You must keep your eyes and ears open, always, for inspiration and wisdom. It will be from various people unaware of their mission most times. Once a happy traveler upon this earth, getting ready to depart to places unseen, spoke sweet words of wisdom and comfort to me. He spoke softly but with conviction and such love. "I don't want to go," he said. "But I have to go." There was not one ounce of regret or trepidation in his words. He continued to speak to me. "Life is wonderful. It is good. It is for living. Although it may be brief, every day should be spent in total living and loving the moments. Don't waste it, not one second." And then he was gone, but his words are still heard. They live and reside within my spirit. They give life, purpose, and meaning to a traveler still upon this earth. Still here. Still watching. Still living. Still listening.

This may not be everybody's belief, and that is okay. But for those that it is, I hope you and everyone will accept it with love. I do not know who is channeling me today, God or Steve, but I am compelled to send this to you today. I know Steve is so settled in somewhere beautiful in heaven, and I suspect he is so happy, just as he always was. In this season of boundless joy, there are those of us still here who have lost a love and a bit of joy. I hope you find comfort in these words. It is the essence of Christmas and indeed of hope and faith. I felt the message was coming from Steve today. It is the absolute truth of which he now has experienced. Believe it and be happy. So here for you today from Steve and God:

> When the perishable has been clothed with the imperishable, and the mortal with immortality, then the saying that is written will come to pass: "Death has been swallowed up in victory." "Where O, Death is your victory? Where O, Death is your sting?" The sting of death is sin and the power of sin is the law. But thanks be to God. He gives us the victory through our Lord Jesus Christ. (1 Cor. 15:54–57 NIV)

Enjoy life free and victorious. Merry Christmas from the Father, the Son, and love from Steve and me.

Occasionally in her thoughts, she was carried back to a tender moment, held firmly in the vault of her heart. It was there for safe keeping, for remembering when she wanted to, when she needed to. He had fixed his gaze upon her in the candlelight of the special dinner set before them. His words would never leave her, although he had to. His time was drawing to an end, and because of that, he had mastered the rare quality of knowing the value of time and truly living in the moment, for the moment. In the brevity of that moment, in that gaze, he spoke beautiful words from his heart. They had meant so much to her then, but as time went by, and the years began to pass, the words gained in monumental value. They were priceless. In the days she had now, she often thought of how important some words are. The heartfelt, genuine words that are spoken to others, especially those we love. She knew firsthand that someday the words may be all someone has to keep in the vault in their heart. So, remember to say them tenderly, lovingly, but above all, say them while you can.

She wondered what Christmas was like beyond the moon, in paradise. Could the citizens of heaven see all the festivities of the season on planet Earth? Were they, the saints forevermore, preparing for the King's birthday among the jewels of paradise? Were they walking upon His streets of gold and within His pearly gates? Did they peer down from above to see their own loved ones who were waiting for the blessed hope as they were scurrying and hurrying about, putting finishing touches on their earthly holiday traditions? And did they wonder if we, the citizens of the planet, remembered what a blessed event the reason for the season is? Did the earth's citizens grasp the truth and meaning and importance of the birth of the Perfect Baby Boy? During this beautiful, special time, she just loved to wonder what was beyond that moon, in a paradise that she dreamed was decorated with the brightest, most beautiful twinkling lights. A paradise that had endless, thunderous choruses of praise to the King by mighty and beautiful angel voices. She wondered, yes, she wondered what Christmas was like beyond the moon in paradise.

I must remind anyone who will listen to stop and think about your life. Journey backward, stopping occasionally to think of how much life you have already lived and how much precious life you have left. The thing is that you cannot know how much precious life you have left, so what you really have is just now, this moment. Please do me and yourself a favor and think about all to this point that you have to be grateful for. The problems of life wax and wane. Things never remain the same forever. There will always be a resolution in time to every problem. Remember also that you can never recover lost time or precious moments. Make your days count. I have had the privilege lately through a widows' support group to read numerous stories of other people's lives and losses. They speak of their precious moments that they hold with a tight grip but also are willing to release and relay with great tenderness and affection as therapy for others. We all know that life here has an expiration date. I used to hate those words "Live like you were dying." They were too sad to think about. Death always seems distant when you are young or healthy or when you are so happy. But it is there, your ever-present enemy. I have gained so much knowledge and insight, compassion, and respect for the tellers of these true, personal, precious moments of their lives and losses. The irony is that they are sharing them with others in a group who have had the same or similar life-changing events, yet the openness, the vulnerability, the raw truth they speak yields strength instead of collapse. There is power in sharing such personal moments. There is strength in knowing your loss is not the only one. There are literally thousands of souls that now know we should all live like we were dying.

Take time to verbally speak the things you are grateful for. Especially let people know that you think about them and really care about them. All the good things we have are great. But it is the living things that make a difference. Friends and family are where the genuine, lasting happiness lies. That is how the precious moments are made. I am hugging each one of you in my thoughts and with my prayers at this very moment. I love you!

You must be one tough person if you are surviving the death of a spouse you loved with all your heart and soul. You are forced to do an abrupt stop to a life you knew and had plans for. You must endure countless "I am so sorry for your loss" from so many well-meaning people. It only drives the stake into your heart even deeper. You suffer endless hours, days, months, and years of depleting loneliness, which is not the same as being alone. You have to get used to being a third or fifth wheel when out with married friends, which only reminds you that you are missing that one person who gave you the emotional security that they still have. When you do venture out and do things by yourself, it is just another reminder that, well, you are by yourself. Holidays are never the same. If you proceed to the dating game, it does not take long for your insecurities or your guilt, or your uncertainty of people, to take over. If you believe in God, your faith is shaken to the core. You waver between blaming God and believing all have a time to die. It is just that you did not expect it when and how it came for your loved one. You spend days trying to decide if it is all worth it anymore. You wish you could have died when your spouse did. For some, you become both mother and father and breadwinner. You juggle all that while still trying to find some peace and healing for yourself. I could go on and on, but with you all, I know I do not have to. At some point, we will all share that life-changing moment that will come to us in varying ways. It will leave a hole in your soul. You will not ever be the same. You will not be who you were, or even who you want to be, but you will be who you *have* to be. That is the way it is. As my sweet husband used to say about his dilemma, "It is what it is."

Loss of a loved one will teach you about compassion. It will teach you to not be judgmental or feel your loss is greater than another's. You will learn to share in another's grief and pain because you are bearing your own. Therefore, you will be able to say with truthfulness that you understand grief and loss. This one thing I know for sure is you will have lived through the worst this life can do to you, and you will still be standing, albeit a little less in stature under the weight of your tears.

Hope: The feeling of expectation and desire for a certain thing to happen; also, a wish, an aim, a goal, a plan, a design. Something to look for, to want, to long for, to dream of.

I had to plan to be a widow for four years, because Steve got his cancer diagnosis four years before he passed away. I had hope back then that things would change, or a cure would be discovered in time to save him. I hoped that God would allow all the prayers of friends across the USA, and friends in Israel leaving prayers tucked in the Western Wall of Jerusalem, to be answered in our favor. Steve never lost hope, but eventually he had to leave. What I want to say here is that although no one should set a time frame on our grief, we ourselves must decide that hope needs to be a part of our life again. If you think about your life, hope has always been a part of it. From hoping for childish things like certain toys for Christmas to hoping for certain people to like you in your teenage years and hoping for certain jobs or promotions in adulthood. We did not always get those things, but I know without a doubt that we always had hope again for something else that meant so much to us. What needs to mean so much to us after our loss is hoping for happiness, hoping for life, for our own life that still has meaning and a purpose and perhaps surprises to fulfill us. Take all the time you need to grieve and heal but start concentrating on just the very meaning of hope, because it is there for each one of us when we are ready to believe it. I remember when my Steve came home from Vietnam in 1968. He told me that after witnessing the death of so many of his brothers in the field, he felt compelled to live life to the fullest, the best, as if he were living it for each of our departed. I think that is the way we need to proceed with our lives, living to the fullest and to the best we can as if we were living it for them. Do what you need to, to get to somewhere you feel strong enough to start hoping, and then never turn loose of it.

Joy and pain weirdly connected in her soul. She could not feel one without the other, and she knew this would be the way it was for the rest of her life.

Everybody who knows me knows how I love the lights. I have several in my home that stay up all the time. Christmas is probably the hardest holiday to go through for anyone who has lost someone they loved, such as a parent, child, or spouse. December gave me the happiest day of my life, December 2, 1966, and it gave me the saddest day of my life, December 8, 2015, but I know that life is still good. Really, it is great, especially in December. I hope to put up lights, maybe today. I just might leave them up all year long. It will be another reminder to all of you to love your life, love the season, and love your people. So, turn on the lights as soon as you can.

Today we finally got the garage totally empty. I got up in the attic, and Missy and I got all my fifty years of Christmas decorations down. Fifty years of really, really, good memories. I found a musical Santa Claus that Steve's mom always had in the kitchen or dining room during the holidays. It was old when I came into the family, so I imagine it was late 1950s or early 1960s. My mind went back to the Barnhart's house, walking in the kitchen door and seeing my mother-in-law sitting at the table drinking coffee and, in the early years, smoking a cigarette. Steve and I would love to sit and talk to her. I loved listening to countless stories of the past, mostly about Steve, because he was the one—the all boy, the fun one. Joy was always a procrastinator, and Steve inherited that trait from her. She was slow to get the tree decorated and even slower wrapping her packages. Usually they got done on Christmas Eve when Nannie and Archie, her mom and stepfather, came in from Houston. She and Nannie would stay up all night drinking coffee, smoking a few cigarettes, wrapping gifts, and as she told me later, just bonding and enjoying each other. As much as she acted like it was a pain to have so many gifts to wrap, I knew that she could have done it a lot earlier. It was just an unspoken tradition that they both cherished. Pulling an all-nighter was just time together, talking about old times and new times. I can remember the smell of coffee and hearing the laughter, and occasionally I could hear the music playing from the very Santa Claus I found today. I have always had this private thing I do since I was married. When I take the tree down each year and put the ornaments away, I always thank the Lord for my family, husband, kids—and all my blessings. But then I ask, "Lord, what will next year bring? What changes will there be? Who will be here, and who will be gone? What will be different when I decorate this tree next year?" Many years, things remained the same. Sometimes the houses changed, but then the years moved along. We lost loved ones. Our wonderful Nannie, then Archie, my grandmothers, Steve's dad, Steve's mom, my sweet daddy, and then our beloved Steve. I did not put up a tree last year. I just did not want to think about what changes might come through the year. This year has been so very hard for me and the kids. There is a great price to pay for loving someone so much. The grief is so much deeper, and I suspect forever. But I really would not change a thing—not one thing. Life is planned for us. I believe that. I am putting that old musical Santa Claus in my home this year. He's kind of worn like me, but he still has his smile, and he still plays music. This Christmas season, I promised myself, I am only going to think about all that I have and all that I have had. I am going to still have my smile, and I will play Santa's music, and I will be loving the beautiful season and my beautiful memories.

My friends have been my "thunder jacket" when the storms were raging around me. With each bolt of lightning news that has invaded my life, and the days of torrential pouring rain of sadness, I was upheld by their phone calls, texts, visits, and most assuredly by their never ceasing prayers for Steve, for me, and for our family. I am forever grateful for the quiet love that they all surrounded me with. It enabled me to float on days I could not pray. When I could not think. I know how much our Lord relishes and loves friendships. He Himself had one when He was among men. His name was Lazarus. I praise Him for the abundance of loving, caring people, including friends, in my life. Oh, how I love you all.

Sometimes tears seem to clear your eyes, and for a brief, few seconds you can see more clearly than ever. I have experienced this occurrence many times. In the middle of my sadness, that is the one thing I notice the most. The physical clearness of my eyesight amid my heartache. I have experienced a lot of tears in the last seven years, but unlike my eyesight, my thought process has not always been clearer after a good cry. On the contrary, many times I just find myself going to sleep and hoping when I wake up all the questions in my mind will be answered and all the problems will be resolved. But life just does not work that way. Tears can speak volumes. There is not one spilled here on earth that is not recorded in heaven. I hope your tears will give you clearer vision to heal your heart or your hurt. My extra prayer is really for all your tears to be tears of joy. Someday I know that prayers will be answered for all of us who belong to Him.

Some memories of the past are held in dreary days and raindrops. Hold fast and wait for the blessed light of tomorrow's sunshine and happier times.

There will be tomorrow. There will be second chances. There will be sunshine, although sometimes through the clouds. She knew that. She had become the rock she needed. The learning had been intense, and the grades had come in. She excelled. She passed in the school of survival. She was changed. She was stronger yet gentler, bruised yet healed, and her scars shone, even glowed in the haze of the moonlight.

I had a great day today. I went to the State Fair of Texas with one of our best friends and his wife, Wayne and Jane. Wayne and Steve traveled together in their work. They became like brothers through the years and had many an adventure together. As usual, we laughed so much, and we talked and shared so many stories about Steve and the many adventures the four of us have had. Laughing is good for the spirit, good for the soul. Sharing the stories made me miss Steve more, but it is so important to keep his memory with us. It is important to remember how special he was. At the end of the day, I told them that lately I feel Steve more and more, and that I hear him talking to me. I said, "It probably sounds crazy or stupid to you." Right then the most beautiful thing happened. Wayne said, "It's not crazy at all, Sandy. I've been wanting to tell you that I feel his presence and talk to Steve all the time now." That was the sweetest way to end my day.

One thing that I love about my group of friends is that all of us are like an endless supply of soothing salve. We are ready to swiftly apply our comfort to any, and all wounded hearts that have gaped open at any given time, day or night.

I am being reflective tonight. I have come a long way. I am learning to not be afraid of tomorrow, expecting bad news or problems. I have learned that we really have little control over life. Maybe the small things, but not the large, life-changing events that hit us out of the blue. I could remind you every day to live your life to the fullest, go after what you want now, take a chance, say the words, do all the things you have put off. Make the dreams come true. I know you will not. You will not until your routine, mundane life is forever changed. Then you realize what joy and happiness really are, and you are not afraid to say the words. You are not afraid to make the changes. You are not afraid of anything anymore, except maybe not having the time to do it all, say it all, change it all, or live it all. From experience, I am saying, "Do not dread tomorrow. Anticipate something good and expect the best. Love with all your heart, the pets, the people, or whatever makes you feel good inside. Don't waste a minute of every single day of your amazing life."

It has gotten to where I can rarely sleep past 5 a.m. Some of the clearest, sweetest thoughts can enter my mind in the absolute stillness of the morning, long before the sun peeks over the edge of my world. I was looking at pictures of my kids and my grandkids and started to tear up. I felt my heart swell, and instantly I thanked God with overwhelming praise for allowing me to have a life, this life. World events, national problems, and turmoil can take a toll on the heart and mind. If you know biblical history, world history, you must be aware that there have always been discord, tragedy, war, and struggles. There have been peaks and valleys, good times and not so good times. There will never be a utopia in this world. We should always strive for betterment but be realistic. We must be visionaries with courage. In-light of all the current tragic events in this country, I have contemplated on some wisdom, some truth, some idea of what message might be learned. I guess for me it has been the resounding, recurring thought that I always have amid these global calamities. The world is never going to be calm or full of peace, nonviolent or friendly, perfect or stress free. Then always God brings to my mind my kids and my grandchildren, my family, and my friends and Him. Not everyone is going to believe in God. That is just the way it is. Free will and personal choices are a slippery slope and should be done with the utmost care. No one knows what tomorrow will bring. As trite as that saying is, it certainly has more of an impact on my thoughts in these times. I say, "Think a lot about those you love. Spend every minute possible with them if you can. If you cannot always do that, just get up early one morning, long before the sun peeks over the edge of your world, and look at their pictures, their smiles. Let your heart swell. Tear up. Thank your Creator." In those moments, you will discover the message He is trying to convey to you through all the world's tragedies.

He has been gone many months now. I did not think I could make it one minute without him. Thank You, Lord for Your faithfulness in-spite of my foolish self. Look his way today, Lord, and tell him we miss him.

What is your quest? It changes as we mature, doesn't it? When time is short, we notice the important things and the simplest things. I remember when my daddy's health was failing, and I was taking him to the doctor one day. He was staring out the window and rather quiet for a while. Then he just started talking about the beauty of the trees. He was seeing and saying how perfect they were in their design. He was transfixed for most of the trip. Then when Steve was nearing his time to leave us, he became enthralled in viewing God's creations, especially the moon. I have come to believe that those special moments were for me, not for the one about to depart this world. I have plenty of time to think now and to analyze. I know God exists. I know that in my immature quests of the past, I was concerned about success, my career, Steve's career, all things in this mortal existence. When you watch someone fading from life, you really start to understand and see the beauty of all that surrounds you. You want to absorb it and hold on to it. If you really look at all the miracles of creation, there is no doubt that they are indeed created. They are not whisked into existence by an explosion or caused by some creature or plant metamorphosis that took billions of years to complete. I was always a control person. I liked being in charge—in charge of the plan, the strategy, the designating of tasks, the finished accomplishment, the results, and the final analysis. Well, I guess age and events can change you, if you allow them to. I rather like my feelings now, knowing what is at stake here. I observe all things around me with more understanding and passion now. I try to feel things deeper. I look at the trees and the moon now with different eyes. I want to experience this experience of life as it was intended for me from God's personal plan designed with my name on it. As far as I know, although I am fading away, I do not have knowledge that it is today. I will observe every leaf of every tree I come across, and I am going to wait to see and marvel at every moon of every night that I have left here. Quests can change. Quests can be enhanced. The benefits are endless, and the perks are eternal.

Today would have been my mom and dad's seventy-third anniversary. Dad passed away in July. It is a sad day for my mom. The first year after you lose someone you have loved is always the hardest. Although it is never the same again, life will and must go on. I am so lucky to have my mom. Always love and treasure your parents. I believe God's promises. One I especially love is to honor your parents so that your life may be long and blessed. Kids are so busy today that I think they do not take time to consider how much their parents love them. I hope that they do not miss the blessing.

Trust in the Lord with all your heart and lean not on your own understanding. In all your ways acknowledge Him and He will make your paths straight. (Proverbs 3:5 NIV)

This was the life-saving message from God to me during the tortuous years of the unknown with Steve's cancer care. It is a message to all of us to put out faith in God only, and even when things don't turn out the way we have prayed for them to, we must believe and trust that God's plans have been set from the moment of our conception. He has given us only so many days to be here in this foreign land. Our home is in heaven with Him. We are here for purposes known only to God. So, whenever you are confused about life and its events, remember the rest of this powerful scripture "lean not on your own understanding" but "in all your ways acknowledge Him and He will make your paths straight."

I still look back and marvel at how the Lord did work and still does in His children's lives. As I said before, He never left my side nor Steve's. The key to a successful life here is a relationship with Christ, a lot of good caring friends, and a loving family. In the aftermath of the loss, God still chose to bless with countless friends and family offering so much love and care that I was overwhelmed. I suppose that God chooses to love us most in these circumstances of loss because He suffered the ultimate loss as a father. He understands the deep love that tears our hearts apart when it happens. All I know today is that no matter what this world brings to us individually, God will never leave you. Seemingly silent at times, but trust me, He will always be there with you and for you.

So, what makes a man a good and special daddy? Whatever is special to the ones he loves, he becomes. He shapes his life around those that depend on him, look to him, and revere him. Some men get it, and some do not. For those who get it, the rewards in this life are the ultimate joy and fulfillment. It is as close to heaven as one can be without really being there. I do not know what they do in heaven on special days of planet Earth, like Father's Day, but just in case, I want Steve to know how much his perfection of being a great dad is still being celebrated. God fixed us so that great love, passionate love, never ends. Being the perfect Father, God knew what we would need the most for trials, hardships, heartache, and loss. Memories and great love abide still in our family. I thank God every day for the man He gave me. We had fun. We had family. We had true love. Happy Daddy's Day, sweet Steve.

Some days I just want to fly to heaven and sit with the Lord. This life has so many unknowns. I have never been afraid of the next day or the future on down the road because I know He is always near and aware and in control of all things in my life and in His world. His world is in a mess and most of us have felt a very unsettling feeling for a long time. Things are not right. Everything seems topsy-turvy. We have been hanging on for a lot of years now, feeling agitated, confused, dismayed, and a bit angry at times. Know that the Lord does not excuse you from stress in this life, but He can calm you to a great extent and encourage you to just be still and reflect on His words and feel His love and assurance. Try to do this today. Be still. Be calm. Reflect on His love for you. When I absolutely do that, then I realize I do not have to fly to heaven just yet. I can sit with the Lord right here where I am.

When I wake up each morning, I am usually looking at the ceiling. I always tell the Lord, "Good morning," first thing, and I thank Him for another day. I rarely have anything on my agenda, and there have been times I have remembered sweet friends who have had losses of loved ones and told me they do not see a reason to even get up in the morning. I refuse to feel that way. Purpose is not always clear, but faith holds my feet steady to the journey's path. So many people out there lose their way. I only know that knowing the Lord reminds me He is the One who knows my way, my purpose. Some days are sad. Some days are long. Some days are full of doubt, but I am grateful for every day that He gives me. I hope no matter what might arise in your day that you will remember the One who loves you and has the right plan and purpose for you. Not every day has to have an agenda. Some days are just for you and Him. I am just letting all of you know that I love you and sincerely appreciate the fact our paths have crossed. Go have a great day and know you are on my mind—as well as on His.

Incredibly happy day today with my best friends of over fifty years. What a blessing it is to have people that long in your life. It is comfort, happiness, and a feeling of security, belonging, contentment, trust, and dependability. It is a heightened sense of joy that makes you realize that your group of classmates are unique and special. We all have made the effort to stay connected or to get connected as soon as we can. That speaks well of us. We do that because we really enjoy one another. We really care for one another. That rarely happens this side of heaven. How lucky we are. Life is swiftly moving along, and we all acknowledge that, but we are determined to keep this thread of lasting relationships weaving and adding to our tapestry of friendship until the last one of us is gone. What a beautiful artwork that will be. For our children and our grandchildren, it will be an example. It will show them we had strong bonds of love for the times we lived as friends, and that life is so much richer, sweeter, and more meaningful when you blend your life with others. So as this day ends, I will say it again how lucky we are, my friends!

The last week has been filled with my grandchildren. As I was having dinner tonight with our college grandkids, we talked about everything from their classes, partying, and marriage to football and roommates. I thought how proud Steve would be of these beautiful kids of ours growing up so fast. I am not sure what people in heaven see or know about us back here. I hope, and most times believe, they see us, but not with remorse or sadness. I hope I am carrying on as he would like for me to. I am counting on him to use all his angelic powers to keep all these kids safe.

There is a need to be quiet at times. A need to listen to your own thoughts in silence. Let them untangle and ease. Go to a place where you can see the mighty moon and stars. Think upon the power of their creation. Go to a place where the only sounds you hear are the gentle wind in the trees, muted croaking frogs and crickets chirping, and your own heartbeat. It is there that the forces of the world will calm. The hurts and the pain of life's complications will fade, even if it is just for a little while. There is such need for rest from life at times. There is such need to lay your burdens away and dwell where there is no load to carry. There is such a need to know yourself and to connect with creation. A need to feel what life was really meant to be. Give me peace, Lord, and lead me to that place, I pray.

Retreat into your own world sometimes. You are not like anyone else. You used to think you were, but you really are not. People come and go, and times change. Feelings wax and wane. There are good times and bad. Life moves on. You either accept it or you refuse to. You take the chance, or you miss the chance. Live in the past or hope for tomorrow. Feel alive or feel nothing. You are the one with you every moment your heart beats and you breathe. The best thing is to like yourself. You are the only you. You are unique and rare. Be happy, celebrate you, celebrate life, love life, and love you. It is the most important decision you will make.

Paint your world any way you choose. I pray you paint it with goodness, positiveness, and love. Be happy for one another, and only want what is best for others. Rejoice when they are happy and hold them in your prayers and thoughts when they are sad and troubled. Enjoy the fleeting days of life, and never fail to recognize the beauty of all of the Lord's creations, be it people, critters, flowers, art, structures, landscape, ocean, or earth. Take time to love it all. Take time to be grateful. Take time to speak the words that others need to hear. Speak the words that the Lord needs to hear. Paint the moon to be full, the sun to be bright, the seasons to be gentle, and life to be all that God meant it to be.

Some good memories for me are those when Steve and I took off to Galveston or Corpus Christi by ourselves. We loved fishing together. He was one of the best. Although I grew up fishing at Lake Texoma with my dad and Uncle Bob, ocean fishing is a bit different, from bait to lines and weights. I paid attention to, listened to, and watched Steve. The exciting thing about dropping a line into the ocean is that you never know what you might reel in. We loved that. I always baited my own hook and even learned to take hard heads off without getting finned. Sometimes I was not sure, but he was always there to do it for me if I needed.

You can learn a lot about a person by watching them fish. Patience and pretty much perfection were what I saw when I watched him. Sometimes he would just look over, wink, and smile at me. Tender, very tender, because no words had to be exchanged. He was saying, "I love you and thank you for enjoying something I love." You cannot play like in a marriage if you want it to be real and good. You must share emotions, feelings, likes, and dislikes. I doubt anyone is totally in love when they walk down the aisle. Love really soaks in a little at a time with the things you share over the years. Honesty is a must. We built a forty-nine-year relationship from scratch. We only knew each other five months when we got married. In five months, we had spent almost every waking minute together. I could not see much wrong with him or the relationship. The sealer of the deal, besides his incredible sense of humor, was that he made me feel secure in every sense of the word. Being so young, we did have our adjustments and ups and downs, but it was never about doubting being loved.

I can counsel anyone on what a good marriage is and what it is not. Sometimes God puts people in the right place at the right time, and they really do fall into His plan. I miss those days of ocean fishing with him, but I have a lot of beautiful memories in my heart to last forever.

Fatalist: One who accepts all things and events as inevitable; submission to fate. Her fatalism helped her to face death with stoic calm. The doctrine that all events are subject to fate or inevitable predetermination.

I am one of these. But instead of fate, I think it is submission to God's predetermined course of life. The thing about it is that God knows since my beginning the things that would occur in my life, from alpha to omega. I'm okay with that, because I don't know the path in front of me and I am still going to live life taking chances, making changes, coordinating moves and strategies, basing the final outcome on my belief that come what may, well, it was just meant to be that way, good or bad. It kind of takes the sting out of mistakes or disappointments and makes me a lot more thankful for the successes and happy results. I am not saying that I am always calm about things falling apart or the unknown, but when I sit and think, and I know that I have done all there is to do on my part, then I have a "faithful calmness," even when there is still no answer or movement on a problem, decision, or desire. I think age has a lot to do with it. I am old enough and have been through enough to know that anxiety and worry never hasten answers or give life's problems more or any clarity.

You may not believe this way, but I do and always have. From the tiniest thing in your life to the biggest, God has known it all since you were conceived. It is kind of awing to think upon. I see no reason to be overly concerned about anything that may happen tomorrow. God's got it. He wrote it down, and all things will happen according to His will and His timing.

It is a serene morning on my balcony. I love seeing my plants thriving. I thought it would be good to have my time with the Lord outside today. I am thankful for everything in my life, but my ultimate joy is having Him with me always. We are all on our way to eternity. He reminds me of that every day. Life here on earth is so very brief. It is really preparation for a forever future. I think a lot lately about purpose. God reminds me that He too has a purpose. It is to love us. Love me. Help me. Guide me. Restore me. And be with me until I meet Him face-to-face. All my strength and purpose are in Him.

When I hear the phrase "We are made in God's image," my mind goes all over the place. I suppose one thing that phrase means is that our appearance, or at least our spiritual being, resembles Him. In anatomy class in nursing school, I became overwhelmed by our construction. It is truly unexplainable in human reasoning. I began to appreciate every face He made. Every fine detail of others' faces, eyes, noses, eyebrows, and mouths I really began to study, and I found something beautiful in everyone. I realized our whole being is in His image, and I began to think on the deeper. Steve and I discussed the heart, feelings, wants, and needs. We agreed that each being was made in need of love, appreciation, and closeness. We both agreed that was part of God Himself that dwelled in everyone. I know one thing for sure: we are all stronger, deeper, happier, safer, and more fulfilled beings with another whose heart and mind share that thought.

When our kids got to the age to date and begin relationships, Steve and I talked about how most young girls want someone to love them, care for them only, feel safe with them, and be their rock and their soul mate. Most young men are looking for trust, loyalty, devotion, and someone to care for them only.

The need for a true close relationship comes from God because that is in Him. Loneliness is why He created man. He could have had angels all day long, but He wanted something a bit higher, something with an actual part of Him in it. Something with the option of free will to choose good or evil, love or hate, truth or lie. It must mean so much to Him each time one of us chooses good, love, and truth.

What I write will not be everyone's cup of tea, and that is okay. I have come to understand that upbringing, choice, location, religion, and circumstances do form us differently. But I really believe, deep down inside us, we are still made with that need to be fulfilled by another's presence in our life, longing for closeness, and a connection. If God felt that way and created man, then I know I am on the right path, and it makes that phrase "we are all created in God's image" ever so more truthful and sweeter. I am hoping that each heart has the experience, the closeness, and the connection that will ease your longings, fill your life with joy and happiness, and cause you to thank God for making that part of Him a part of you.

It was early in the morning, and as had been the custom lately, I could not sleep. It had been two weeks since Steve left us. I lay down on the couch in the den, where he had been lying for so many weeks before. I think I was trying to absorb any of him that might still be there. Then I went to the coat closet and stuck my hand in the pockets of his jacket. There were some Kleenex, a grape sucker, and two peppermints. I began to cry, thinking that it had only been a few weeks ago that he had that jacket on. I put it on for a little while and sat in the darkness, talking to the Lord.

Grieving is a hard thing. You have a million people around you, yet the loneliness consumes you. Forty-nine years of love, laughter, and memories cannot dissipate in two weeks, two months, or two years, nor do I want it to. I just want the new normal to start to ease some of the sadness. The new routine to take my mind forward. I will be okay, and I certainly do not want Steve back in the condition he left us. I get the assurance from the Lord that Steve is well, good, and busy for now. I believe Steve is aware of the unbelievable love and support he had from so many people, and he is aware of those same people now providing the same for me and the kids. God is good. I know that even in the midst of deep sorrow. Some people say that I am strong. No, not by myself. I looked up the definition of strength and there are three. I like this one that says, "the number of people comprising a group; typically an army." So, you see, I do not have the strength you all say you see in me alone. The strength is the Lord and you and me—a team, an army. Isn't that what God intended? For us to care that much for each other. And with Him in the mix, the strength can eventually overcome anything this world throws at us. I tell you once again that I love you all. You are my army of strength.

Time does not really make things better. I am just telling you so that you will be prepared. A lot of things you do will be done just going through the motions. You keep it going for everyone else, for appearances. What are you going to do? Just stop? I remember when a good friend lost his son. At the family night when I hugged him, he said he was now looking forward to when he could join him in heaven. I remember my granny telling me that when my grandfather died suddenly at the age of forty-two, leaving her with eleven children to raise, she wanted to go with him to heaven that very day. I have a sweet family member who lost her son in Afghanistan. I read her posts and feel her pain. She longs to be with him again. Then there is my sweet mom in her nineties ready to move on "home" to be with my daddy. I love life. I really do. But life is hard sometimes, and sometimes you just do not want to do it. You must have strong faith in God and believe He controls all things, all lives, and believe He has a purpose for even the hard things in life. Really that is all that will get you through. I think it is called hope. When you have that kind of faith, God will give you hope. It does not take away the hard things of life, it does not even change your mood sometimes, but hope is always in the back of your mind. This little word *hope* has great power if you believe in it. I do. My days are not the same. My life is not the same, but even on my saddest days, I hold out for hope. Life is going to continue. The earth is going to continue to spin. Time will continue to tick away. We all will experience loss and some hard times. It is just that circle of life. I can get through it. You can get through it. Hope is why I can get up each day and continue to continue. I have hope that God still has a purpose for me. I have hope that I can still continue to enjoy my kids and grandkids. I have hope that there are many more good times to spend with my friends. In-spite of all the turmoil, hope is what really keeps the world going. I am not sure the world understands this, but I do. Hope equals God. Be sure and tell people you love them, take time to enjoy life and really live, and always hold out for hope no matter what.

Do not feel sorry for yourself, have regrets, or dwell on the negative or the past. Let good memories roll through, but do not get caught up in what-ifs or the should-haves or could-haves. If things were meant to be, they would be. Just arise with a thankful, grateful heart and sweet thoughts that fill your head, and sweet words that roll off your tongue. Remember that life is a gift, and we all have an expiration date. Live like there is no tomorrow. Have a clean conscience. Keep the past tucked neatly back where it belongs. Keep eyes forward and marching onward, loving yourself and all those who matter.

In my Steve's words, and I could not have said it better, "It is what it is." Remember that in this life, no matter what happens. Just because you do not want something to be or don't want to face something, it won't change it. After I faced what we had to face and dealt with it, it became easier to accept anything else in my life. God does not always work things out like we hope. He does not always heal on this side, save a relationship, or give you the job you were hoping for, but He is still God and He is still in control. And anything that happens, well, it just is what it is.

Urgency: 1. Importance requiring swift action 2. An earnest and persistent quality; insistence.

So here I am, the description that defines the way I live. I have always felt an urgency about life. The need to do it all and do it all quickly. To fulfill the boundless callings of this beautiful gift of awareness and living. It was pure joy and a blessing having a partner who had that same drive and desire to live like there was no tomorrow. Say all the words and express all the heart tells you to on any given day before that day is over. God's words about the brevity of life are repeated in His scriptures. You need to heed the message of the importance of limited time that He so often repeats. I, for one, will not leave this earth without being spent of every ounce of living. I will say the words daily that I feel led to speak. I will love and demonstrate that passion for people and things in the moments of every day I am here. Why would you do otherwise? Why would you save up the feelings, the love, the desires, the talents, or the opportunities that reside within you?

I once heard a speaker talk about the joys and blessings God has for each of us. He spoke of the "closets in heaven" that contain good things God intends for us. We each have a separate one with our name on it, full of things of delight that the Lord has intended specifically for each one of us. The thing about it is you must ask for those blessings. God wants to hear from us. It is just you, and Him talking about your wants and needs. He will freely give you, from your closet, what you need and sometimes, if for your good, what you want. He wants that communication with you— just you and Him. I do it often. My wants and needs are not really that extravagant. I know without a doubt that my thank-you to God for such blessings from my closet is not to waste one moment of precious time on my pilgrimage here on earth and to use and express the feelings He has laid within my heart and soul to other pilgrims on the journey. If there is one thing you think on, think about living life higher and bolder, deeper and richer, expressing all the truth within you—as if there were no tomorrow.

They say when you die that your whole life flashes before you. I hope so. I want to see every precious, beautiful moment again.

Sometimes I feel lost, even though I know where I am. Sometimes I need assurance often, even though I know for sure. Sometimes I need to be hugged and held, even though I know I am loved. Sometimes I feel sad, even though I feel happiness again. Sometimes I just need to remember how valuable I am when I am making others feel their own worth. Sometimes I just need silence amid the noisy chaos in my mind. Sometimes I just feel lost, even though I know where I am.

God bless all those who come into our lives and make our life a better place than it was before. Those who give us comfort in our sadness and have a way of making us smile. Those who care. Those who love us. Those who are there for us. Thank You, God, for those You sent into our lives. God, please bless them mightily.

We all have struggles, with ourselves mainly. We struggle to move forward and find new happiness or new love. But to live is to look ahead. My prayer for every aching heart everywhere is not to stand still. Look ahead and build the new.

Hug a little longer; love a little deeper. Say what you mean and mean what you say to those you hold so dear. Do not waste another minute on the trivial. Make every moment count because they all are so precious. Be thankful to the Lord always. He has given life to you and provided the Way to reach Him. Do not miss the directions.

I remember when I was very, young and being at my grandmother's house in Van Alstyne. On a warm, summer night, we would throw a quilt out on the front lawn and lie under the stars of a big Texas sky. Gazing up as a child, I really did not even know then what to dream for or about, but I remember the good feeling I had looking up into the heavens. I heard talk on those nights by the grownups about the past and all the changes. I knew nothing of that because my only thoughts as a child were on the now. I was just beginning to create my past on those warm Texas nights in a little country town. Now I kind of long for a quilt thrown out on the front lawn under the stars, gazing up into the heavens, thinking of times gone by and all the changes. Some memories are special. Those are the ones that will never leave you.

Do not get so wrapped up in your "religion" that you become unreal. It is okay for your flaws to show sometimes. God's grace, mercy, and love become illuminated in a "real person" and to the eyes of another "real person" struggling with their worth. Christ dwells outside the church walls as well as within. And sometimes outside those walls, He is a lot more recognizable.

We are most divine when we love. We are most pure when we believe. We are most happy doing both.

Yesterday is old news with a pile of things not accomplished and stale thoughts. And tomorrow? Well, who knows if you will get there? Procrastination is just a slow death to living. When is the right time? Right now, always. Say the words, spend the time, make the call, do the trip, and give the kiss. Exhaust every ounce of life out of you this day. When you have no more days, be the thought, the picture, the sweet memory in someone else's today. That is the only legacy that is great. To leave a small bit of yourself with others. That is the Nobel Prize of life.

Go on and hit me with your best shot. These words we utter in defiance of being thrashed and conquered by some of life's cruelest shots. I do not feel that I am unique or stronger or anything special. I really do not. Early on, I understood that life is not easy. It never was meant to be. Where are the lessons learned and the strengths to share if you never experience the unrelenting ebbs and flows of this earthly life? Life was meant to be shared, to touch lives and to be touched by other lives. Life was meant to be contemplated yet to be lived with reckless abandon. Some of the best of life is from taking chances, going with your gut, going out on a limb, and throwing caution to the wind. I learned to live that way from an excellent instructor. My life has been molded almost solely by him. Totally happy was he. I dwell in the realm of taking chances. Do it now. Why wait? Taking chances gets you knowledge. It clears your mind. Taking the chance may mean you get or accomplish exactly what you wanted, or it may mean you do not get exactly what you wanted. But at least you know one way or another. Every day should be a "warrior day" for all of us. Life is a jungle. We begin every day on the edge of the thick, dense foliage of unseen life ahead. Forge ahead. Meet life head on. You take control. You take the chances. You be the conqueror. You, out there reading this, give life *your* best shot. You be the warrior today.

Let your feelings soak deeply into your soul,

The only way to truly live, to be whole.

We were designed to love and appreciate

Every good thing our Master did create.

Set your eyes on oceans, mountains, and moon,

And your spirit will soar and sing a grateful tune.

Life is meant for us all to be aware

Of how much for us our Creator cares.

His blessings of life are always there in view.

Open your eyes, your heart; He gives the choice to you.

Just give me truth. Just give me honesty. Give me the real people. Ones who can be funny and serious. Ones who know themselves and are not full of themselves. Give me genuineness. Give me a true heart, no fakeness or flakiness, no spinning or whirling. No hot and cold. Just give me consistency. No games, no players, no room for that. No time for that. Just give me the truth. Just give me the honesty. Give me the real people. These are just some of my observations of life and needs on the downhill slope of time on planet Earth.

Hope, dream, and believe. Desire the beauty in life and the purposes designed for you. Strive to be available for whatever pulls at your heart and speaks to your mind. Those are the true callings worth paying attention to. Those are the things of God's destiny for you. The moon once heeded the command of Almighty God and fulfilled its reason and worth. And now completely satisfied, it hangs in God's universe doing exactly what it was meant to do.

Time is short. If you miss someone, call them. If you love them, tell them. If you want to spend time with someone, show up and do it. These words will mean more when you experience great loss, one that cannot be recovered. We cannot control time. When the moments are there, you had better act upon them. Sometimes that is the very last opportunity you will ever have.

The shattered, broken heart resurrected is stronger, wiser, and deeper than ever before. When the bleeding subsides and the healing begins, the scars that form make a beautiful texture to life. There is more appreciation, more recognition of importance, and more measuring the worth of moments. Though the memories of the pain and sorrow reside within the scars, those scars can encourage the heart to find new purpose, new happiness, a new beat. Living with a scarred heart is opportunity to understand life, to understand others, to have compassion and grace, and to value the pain endured as something special that makes the resurrected, scarred heart more beautiful than ever before.

There is a constant conflict within me. Some days I have strength and optimism and see ahead. And others, I just do not see it. Checking out would be a relief. No matter how hard you try, no matter how busy you stay, no matter how much you love others, no matter how much you preach and write about moving forward, loving life and depending on the Lord, some days you just can't get there. You just cannot see anything but disappointments, heartaches, uncertainty, and the life you used to know. I suppose the darkness is winning today, maybe because it is Monday. Maybe it is a different pull of gravity on my emotions due to the eclipse. Maybe it is just my reality from here on out. We have the right to feel this way some days—we people who have lost someone we love so deeply. The pieces of your heart are gone forever, and the heart never beats the same again. Some days, it barely beats at all. Sunshine and shadows both fall on us. Only a few will bare their souls and give warning to others of their impending shady days. Bask in the light while you may and hold on to it for as long as possible.

For someone who has been on speed dial and a microwave world forever, it is one of the hardest things to do to step back, slow down, wait, trust, and not worry. I am not perfect at this thing, one day at a time, but I want to be and am trying to be. So much can happen in a day or not happen in a day. I am still learning about faith.

There is a past to every life lived, a yesterday, or years of yesterdays. A past of any length is not the deciding definition of life, for we are changing minute by minute. We are new with each dawning day. Do not stay in the past if you are still living and loving life. We have come through many yesterdays, bringing with us the knowledge we need to begin anew each day, to begin it in a new way. The past teaches, but the past expects you will not stay. Take what you need, but do not dwell or become burdened by the past. For you have fresh, uncharted paths to venture upon, and many new faces to see, and beautiful new loves to find. Relish the sunshine of opportunity each morning and bid goodbye to the moon of the evening as it closes the day and drifts into the past.

The poet, the songwriter, and the author never rest. The words fill the head and burden the heart to be expressed. And when the thoughts are finally penned, the words fill the head again.

Earth, wind, fire, and water all beckon us in their own way. Fields of flowers, gentle breezes, flickering flames, and running brooks know we long for their peace and their power, and they are willing to freely share with us. If we would only take the time to absorb their presence and beauty.

Life unfolds like a present some days. Joy and memories reside in a grateful heart. You must value the minutes you are given, for they are fleeting and can never be reclaimed. Look into the eyes of everyone you speak to. See deeply into their hearts and sense their needs, their dreams, and be amazed at their uniqueness and beauty. We are all but travelers upon earth's soil, searching for some direction and purpose. Be kind and gentle, and honest with all you meet. Those you choose to keep, love them with care, and love them deeply. Make yourself a permanent brand upon their mind so that when they need to, they may linger in the warmth of the affection you bestowed. Be a peacemaker. Be a gentle light that draws many weary ones to you, so that the difference they are seeking may be found in you.

Be contagious. Let your spirit be infectious. When you walk into a room of people, be the standout, not for your looks or eloquent voice but for your happy spirit and satisfied soul. Be a bright light to break through another's clouds. Have eyes that seek out one who needs you, and then be there. Have ears to hear even silent pleas for love and understanding. Have arms that extend in truth to hug another. Give them unconditional love. Taste the sweet and bitter of life without regret and share your experiences and knowledge lovingly to a hurting soul needing to be encouraged. Smell the sweet fragrance of forgiveness because it is your freedom. Leave your glitter wherever you can. Radiate the positiveness of our Lord and His wonderful life. We are all but brief burning candles of light put here for purposes bigger than ourselves. Find yours, live it, and love it until all your candle has been used and you have ignited many new wicks of purpose of your brothers and sisters.

If I could fly away, where would I fly to? Would I just let the winds carry me where they may, or would I steer my own course? To be free, to be above the fray, to have no fear. Just to float with the clouds and to soar with the eagles. Oh, to be lifted higher and higher as a feather caught up in a current. Freedom, sweet freedom ... To drift with no plan or to wing where the heart guides. If I could fly away, where would I fly to?

Love is not the word spoken, for words fall short of actions. It is the doing, the showing, the touching, or the holding. Actions convey truth without a single word uttered. You must be so very willing to lift love to movement and meaningful actions; otherwise, it will fade and die. Love must be nurtured with presence and pruned of boredom and watered with sweet surprises. A heart that sees and feels love beats with unyielding desire and gains passion with each tender deed, filing away those moments as precious treasures forevermore.

Always be happy for others when goodness, peace, and happiness are evident in their lives. For you do not know the heartaches, the pain, the confusion, the struggles, or their deepest agonies endured to get to a resting place of calm and hope in their personal journey. It matters not your judgment or opinion, for their lives, circumstances, feelings, and heart are not yours. Be wary of issuing criticism, lest you be all alone when your trials and life's calamities befall you. And they will. Love with a pure heart, and love with genuine compassion. Love as our perfect example did. The brevity of life makes it imperative to spend our time in uplifting each other.

Music is medicinal. It is therapy. It speaks the words we feel and makes them poetry that causes us to feel all the emotions of life. Happy, painful, reflective, hopeful, nostalgic—the important thing is that music makes us feel something. The heart needs music when it needs to be healed. Play the music every day.

Let me drift upon the water ever so gently as I think about my life. Days long gone that molded me, blessed me, taught me. Days of stress and sadness that molded me, blessed me, taught me. Days of healing and discovery and changing. Praying that they mold me, bless me, teach me. Let me drift upon the water ever so gently.

She floated between emotions. She was fragile and somewhat insecure, never really knowing or feeling her worth. If she let you in, she would never let you go. When she gave you her heart, you had all of it. She had an uncanny way of recognizing and culling out pretentious humans. To her, every moment was valuable, never to be wasted on anything that was not real. She longed for security, but she knew that security was always fickle and fleeting. The hurts she felt were deep, but she would not speak of them. For who would listen? Who would care? She chose instead to just float between emotions.

I think too deeply most days. I analyze stuff way too much. I am constantly critical of myself. I second-guess a lot of things I say or do. And, in-spite of all that, God says to me, "Just be still and know that I am God, and that I love you." And then He says, "Look around you." And when I do, it is evident that I am surrounded by the most wonderful friends. I am grateful for all of you. For your encouragement, your love, your support, and your genuineness. In some of my darkest days, you all held out the light to get me to God's saving path. Life really is not complicated. Life is wrapped up in one word: love. Love for one another. And in that love comes every kind of genuine care and action possible. There is such a bond that is forged in friendships that have weathered the tough times. They are the golden forever kind. They never erode or fade. They gain in strength with the years and the happenings and always sharing the love.

If I could only give you one valuable bit of knowledge that I know to be absolute truth, I would tell you to choose your words wisely if they are to be spoken aloud. They are the most powerful things that we possess. They can be weapons set to destroy, hurt, or maim. They can be healers to a hurting soul longing for comfort; they can be tender and spoken only to the one lover you are forever connected to. They can be full of praise spoken to the One you worship as your Creator and God. They can also be the words in your thoughts to yourself when you feel doubts or when you have questions. When you think about what you should say in this situation or that situation or when you have been hurt or feel unappreciated, misunderstood, or unloved. It is these words that are best kept silent All things good, bad, misunderstood, or unappreciated do pass. Spoken words can never be taken back and when said in anger or hurt are seldom forgotten. Something repaired is never as strong as something whole.

My head is full of thoughts. My heart is full of messages. I really need a break, Lord.

Go to the countryside where you can think, away from the hubbub and noise. Think deeply about all the life you have lived and all the love you have loved, all the memories you have made, all the pleasures you have partaken of, all the dawns and sunsets you have seen, and all the starry skies and moonlit nights you have enjoyed. Dwell on the blessings of life amid the beauty of God's landscape. Let loose the things that weigh you down. Let them drift up and away into the baby-blue country sky and disappear behind the marshmallow clouds. Go to the countryside, feel the freedom, and think of all the blessings of your life.

At the end of the day, I am always thankful for one more day. One more opportunity to gather up some happenings and roll them into knowledge or memories or joy. Not every day feels that way, but it is important to me to find one of the above before nightfall. I try because some of those that I have loved and are not here now loved this life so much, and they taught me how important living is, even the ordinary days. There is much joy in the mundane, routine, nothing-going-on days. Regardless of how we feel, each day is for a reason, and as trite as it sounds, it is a gift for us and possibly for someone near us. My heart keeps striving for more happiness. I want more happenings, more memories, and more joy. What I have gathered in the past from ordinary days is sweet. Sometimes its memories hurt my tender heart, but it is all worth it. Always changing, always being molded by every day we live. Finding joy, sometimes through tears, but always thankful for one more day.

Simple and uncomplicated joys of life are the ones that we will dwell on in our golden years. A small garden planted by our own hands, tended to with love and anticipation, and a little harvest that gave us a few good meals. It is life's ordinary days that weave the magical memories that are more precious than silver or gold.

You cannot know the future. You cannot live life before it gets to you. So, we walk with faith day-to-day without even realizing it. Blindly we forge ahead, making our plans, going here and there like ants on a hill. As the years mount up and we look back at all the days we have been given, it is then that we realize how precious life is. That it is indeed better not to have all the answers to life. It is better not to know how the mysteries of the universe work but to experience it as our Creator planned, as a gift that we open every day, depending on Him to lead and to take care of all our tomorrows.

May your days always feel like sunshine and moonbeams.

May your life always be filled with passion and dreams.

May you always speak softly with kindness and truth.

And may you always love tenderly as you did in your youth

So that when the winds of age do reach your door,

You will be satisfied with warm memories forevermore.

Fill your heart with happiness. Be thankful for where you are now. Do not think too deeply lest you ruin the moment of content. Expect nothing yet give everything. Make no apologies for what you feel. Be bold in living life. Make a difference in one person's life. See how good it feels, then do it again. Live honestly, then you will have no regrets, and yes, love full out with the intensity your heart whispers to you. In the quiet moments, dwell on how fortunate you are to be who you are and where you are. Blessed beyond measure.

Life can be troublesome and sad sometimes, but if you keep the faith, pray, and believe life is good and God is good, He can restore and heal anything. He will bring you to the right destiny.

As you point yourself ahead, all your past will try to weigh you down, all the reminders of good and bad things. But life was not designed to stay in one place, stuck in the best or worst of events. It is always moving, flowing, never stopping to amass any treasures of life. We are all on a trek in this world. So, although we all travel together, we travel differently with suitcases full of varying meanings and purposes. The journeys intersect at times, and we see other parts of life that, although not our own, cause us to pause ever so slightly and take note. We learn best from each other, not only about others but sometimes about ourselves. Travel, my friends, always aware of the possible brevity of your journey and the importance of every day's scenery and pilgrims you meet. Most of all, keep moving forward. Nothing is accomplished from regrets of the past, but only in the opportunities that lie before you this day.

Elevate yourself today. Look at who you are and all you have accomplished, endured, and come through. There will never be another you. Learn to like who you are and where you have come from. Give thanks for your unique construction. Your heart beats. You are alive. You have people who love you and would not be happy without your presence on this earth. You have touched many, unknowingly sometimes. Love who God has given you. Never miss an opportunity to tell someone how much they mean to you. Elevate them. One word of kindness, appreciation, or praise may be all they need to feel worthy. Look deep within yourself. Review your life. May all your hurts heal. May all the best times be illuminated. May the sunshine always shine on you. May joy, peace, and thankfulness rule you. You are my joy and my happiness. You have saved me many times in my grief, loneliness, and sadness. You give my life purpose and meaning. Always remember that I love you.

Love your life. Embrace where you are. Trust and believe. Your journey is not over.

If I could advise you using my journey, I would say that you must be your own sounding board, your own decider of how you want your life to be. No matter what may befall you, go easy on yourself. Make the pressure light. Mull things over, including your words, your thoughts, and your actions, before you act upon them. Once you understand that you are just a human being with flaws and mistakes and baggage in tow, then you will learn to be kinder and thoughtful to others you meet with flaws, mistakes, and baggage in tow. Practice kindness. Practice peace. Practice love. Happy is the one who not only sees the sun rise but also feels the worth of another day, another chance to live.

"Someday they will understand," she said, "how a heart can hurt so badly yet not stop beating."

"Someday they will understand," she said, "how difficult making changes can be that save your very life."

"Someday they will understand," she said, "that God directs your steps when you are His child and all alone."

"Someday they will understand," she said, "that after great loss, you can be happy again, just differently."

"Someday they will understand," she said, "when it happens to them."

Her heart overflowed,

Yet it felt empty.

Remembrances and emotions

Had left it bruised.

Yet as if addicted,

She craved the pain

To live again,

To feel again,

To matter again.

Not only do the same stars and moon shine down on all of us everywhere on earth, but those on the other side see that beauty from a ringside seat with the Creator Himself. That is what I think when I look up into the heavens at night and see the beauty thereof. I feel a closeness to the one I loved so much, and I feel he is saying, "I see you. I know where you are. I am good. I am happy. I am waiting." That elevates and enhances the beauty of the nighttime sky beyond my mind's imagination and my heart's desire.

The enjoyment of life is making memories. No one ever thinks about that in their youth, yet that early gathering of memorable moments creates some of the sweetest of life. Bonds that run deep and forever are the strength that you will depend on one day down the road. Some memories are good, and some may not be so good, but they all sculpt us into the beautiful masterpiece that is revealed in our golden years.

The cold winds of life blow stronger these days,

Stinging you deeply in such piercing ways.

Precious people here a minute ago

Now gone, and it leaves us missing them so.

Valuable moments, live them, everyone.

Soak up what you can until day is done.

The satisfied soul knows the worth of real love.

Its contentment lies in truths from above.

When those winds blow upon you, and they will,

Seek a shelter with loving arms to hold you until

You can handle life as it is now going to be,

With the same courage and strength, but differently.

She felt alone a lot of the time. She was not, but there was always this sense of isolation within. No one really understood her feelings, her darkness at times. Not even her. She kept waiting for this epiphany, this divine revelation for direction, meaning, and purpose. She was not hopeless, for she had been delivered from herself and her deep, internal struggles before. She held on only by her faith, even if it was by one single, fragile thread. That fragile thread was reinforced from somewhere. She chose to believe it was the One True Living God that held her in the balance and that He would never let her fall. She was different. She was complicated, yet her heart was open, always seeking the closeness and the understanding that always seemed to elude her.

Sadness swept over her like a silent breeze. From where it came, she did not know. It swirled her thoughts and made her heart heavy, yet she knew it would not last forever. It moved at its own will on the days when her life was gray and gloomy, but she had learned that the melancholy winds would pass in time and happiness as vibrant as a summer morning would appear and restore her heart and mind. She whispered to herself, "Hang on. Just hang on. Life is ever-changing, windy, stormy, sunny, and calm. Just weather the difficult, knowing the sun is not ever hidden forever."

Isn't it revolutionary when you realize how much something impacted your life? My entire married life, from beginning to end, was affected by the Vietnam War. Little did I know that would be the case at the tender age of eighteen. Life can make you bitter or better. Steve always chose the high road. Sending out some love, respect, and admiration to all Vietnam War veterans. I just had you guys on my mind and tonight.

I am in the waves today, trying to stay afloat. Sadness ebbs and flows just like the tide. For future widows and widowers, if you have a best friend as a spouse, make a mental note of the following. When you are alone for good, the undertow of the waves can overtake you at any time. When that happens, you will have to start all over again where it is shallow, and you can see the bottom. You must be the one to save yourself from the current when it beckons you out too far in your endless sea of thoughts and memories.

Nothing will activate your mind to deeper thought than grief. Sometimes you cannot turn off the thoughts, the ones you really do not want to reflect on. The heart is busy hurting, while the brain is having to do the tough stuff. It occurred to me that amid all the living we do from the onset of birth, it is simply preparation for when we will experience grief. Grief is the ultimate test of strength for human endurance. How you have faced life is exactly how you will face grief.

Life is a balancing act from start to finish. Some days will be heavy, and some will be light. Proceed with no expectations but with anticipation of discovery and changes. Life will not stay predictable forever. Enjoy the quiet days and garner strength and wisdom for life's turbulent times. The deeper the downs, the loftier the highs.

Moonlight on the water,

Starlight in the sky,

God shares these things of beauty

For every human eye.

I'll never take for granted

The wonders that are free.

Many times, within my heart,

I feel they're just for me.

Learning to forgive when you are hurt is one of the toughest tests God gives. It can only be done when you push self aside and weigh the losses. Life has so many pitfalls. You will be learning every day you are here, up until your very last breath on planet Earth.

Our private tears are so tender, so genuine, so special. Each one is speaking to God, and only He understands the language they speak.

Sometimes sleep just does not come. The mind is powerful. It can whirl a million thoughts at a time like arrows directed at every emotion you possess. You know what? Life is complicated at times. Nothing—and I repeat, nothing—is more important than living full out and being happy for as long as you possibly can. Whatever that may be, and, if it is above the law. You truly put things in perspective when you have watched, up close and personal, life end for someone you love. Facing their mortality forces you to face your own. I am happy for anyone who chooses after a time to take any path that brings them to happiness and healing. Some say I have changed. It is my circumstances that changed. I am the same person. Circumstances forced me to change directions after heading on the same course for so long. You lose some people sometimes when you find new happiness. But you must remember that this is about *you* finding new life and reasons to get up every day. They have not been in your shoes. I am truly thankful for my Lord, Jesus Christ. He has been my faithful friend and companion through my whirlwind of changes. It is by His grace and direction that I have found my way out of the dark tunnel. Life is always going to change, and sometimes not for good, and then sometimes its changes are exquisite. Every minute you are given to live is a gift to you and to many others you may not even be aware of. Take hold of all your moments, keeping in mind that neither the good ones nor the bad ones last forever. Just be grateful for all of them.

Just float. Just divest of the world's problems and your worries. Dwell on all that you know is good. Leave the hubbub and go where your mind and your heart can communicate on what is best and positive and happy for you. Drift a while in thought, only letting in that which is peaceful and calm. Uplift yourself, and do not let happiness be dependent on circumstances or people. Replace wavering happiness with joy. For true joy is unyielding power over happiness, which can crumble in an instant. Delve into yourself and find that which feels right, that feels like it fits. Practice kindness and compassion and have strength in the knowledge of who you are, where you came from, your uniqueness, and in the silence of meditating with your Creator. Believe in your abilities, your talents, and your worth. Each face, each body, each soul is a masterpiece. One of a kind. Value yourself as He did when He designed you on a heavenly blueprint. There was no carbon paper, and there was no transference of His draft of you. Every thought of His at that moment was directed to only you and to molding you into a perfect plan. And even now you remain a priority to Him. Knowing all that, you should believe even more in yourself. Believe in your capabilities, and believe in your value, for you are priceless.

Sometimes I do not feel my worth. Some days are just that way, you know. There will be times when you give of yourself until it hurts. Not really doing it expecting anything in return, but if you are being perfectly honest about it all, sometimes you *would* like something in return. A tiny thing, not of monetary value. Perhaps a hug, perhaps a kiss, perhaps a phone call, perhaps just a word from someone that lets you know your value to them. To know you are important, even if it is just for a moment. Don't ever forget to take the opportunity to let people know how much you love and appreciate them. Life is short. Real life is made up of moments with others, making memories, reliving memories, always edifying each other. That is literally what we all need on any given day: a golden gift that will not tarnish. Please pass it on.

They looked at her and could not see

Just how broken a heart could be.

But in the evening, so calm and fair,

The moon did rise to say, "I care."

He bathed her in his muted light

As gentle winds kissed her goodnight.

Sleep would come to ease her soon,

Protected, guarded by her faithful moon.

Sometimes late at night, all the bad thoughts and doubts disturb your sleep and you find yourself awake. You may be sitting in front of your Facebook friends, some still awake too. I know the mind is the most complicated thing ever created. It is a storehouse of every moment, every feeling, every good or bad event of your life, and it seems it does the best and nosiest display of all the information it stores in the wee hours of any given morning. So here I am, jumbled thought and emotions running rampant. I have reached a summit in my life, and as I look back on that rocky, often quagmire of a road I just finished, I cannot believe I survived intact. And although I am still standing at this summit, my mind seems to enjoy hurling all the negative thoughts of things that are over and cannot be changed. It is a constant battle that we have with this huge storehouse in our head. Oh, I know. When daylight comes, this fickle friend will pull out all the lollipop and roses thoughts and memories, and tonight's tears and hurts will evaporate until another restless evening rears its ugly head. Two thoughts stick in my mind. One is a song from *Annie*. "Tomorrow, tomorrow, there's always tomorrow." Well, let us hope so. Then there is a quote by Ernest Hemingway:

> Try to learn to breathe deeply, really to taste food when you eat, and when you sleep, really sleep. Try as much as possible to be wholly alive with all your might. And when you laugh, laugh like hell, and when you get angry get good and angry. Try to be alive. You will be dead soon enough.

Pretty much says it all. Being alive is a good thing, and really our storehouse mind is a great thing. It is just a carefully preserved movie reel of your life, set to roll anytime it wants. We must remember two things when it starts to roll. That there is tomorrow, when the sun will come out and things look differently, and most of all, as Ernest put it, just really live your life, deeply, fully with passion. Thwart the negative stuff. Chalk it up to learning. Take it in stride, and do not get defeated by the past you cannot change, especially at 2 a.m. Think of ocean waves and calm summer nights and cool autumn days, and drift back to sleep.

This widow girl decided to get out today, or at least I thought I would. I got dressed. I put on my sweater and shoes and took the elevator downstairs. I got my mail and took the hallway door to my garage. I stood there on the step in the hall for about three solid minutes and then asked myself, "Where you going to go?" It just did not seem like a good idea at that point. So, I came back upstairs. Funny how your mind will not let you rest sometimes. On days like this, Steve and I would go downtown Grapevine and just walk around. We would get a Margarita or two and sit on the patio of our favorite Mexican food place and people watch. We would just enjoy being together, savoring moments. I am telling you this because it is all part of the journey. You will have days that you are sailing, and you are the captain, and you will have days you are in the submarine and it's not coming to the surface at the moment. It will be okay. Today I am just adjusting my compass.

I heard this somewhere: "God has perfect timing, never early, never late. It takes a little patience and faith, but it's worth the wait."

When you are in the darkness for any length of time, it is hard to believe this much less trust this. I have spent many a night lately mad at God. My sweet mom raised an eyebrow when I told her that I was mad at God. But it is true, and if you are honest with yourself, then you will have to admit that you have been there too. Here is one thing that I love so much about our heavenly Father: He is bigger than any feelings that you will encounter. He loves, in-spite of our feelings, because He sees the whole picture. Not just the moment, but from beginning to end of every life that He has allowed to be. I relate it to how, as teens, your kids get so angry with you over a decision you have made regarding them, and they slam their bedroom door as they pout, hating you because the decision was not what they wanted. Yet a few years down the road, they are throwing their arms around you, loving you to their brink, and then actually telling you. I know I am a teenager sometimes in my Father's eyes. I am on a road that is difficult at times, shadowy, scary, filled with some bitter disappointments. But also filled with indescribable joys, like when my kids throw their arms around me and tell me they love me. Yes, faith and patience, I am learning in my "golden teenage" years with God, can and will bring wonderful rewards.

I put Christmas lights up today. I just wanted to be festive, bright, and happy. I had a lot of random thoughts going on, as that is how my mind works lately. Steve and I always did everything together. He was not a hunter or a golfer. Not a weekend-with-the-guys kind of guy. Other than pigeon shows once or twice a year, he was just always there, with me. We really, *really* enjoyed each other. We trusted each other. We respected each other. We loved each other.

I could not get the fact that he had to leave as he did out of my mind today. There are only two big things he has done without me in forty-nine years: go to Vietnam to serve this country in war and leave this world for heaven. I kept thinking today, *He's already there. He's already made that journey that nobody really knows about.* No one knows how you get there or what transpires during your heaven-bound travel. It was just a strange day. I kept feeling like he was here with me. I felt him tell me not to worry, that when it was my time, he would be there along with the Lord to lead me home. It would have been so like him, because he was the most protective guy ever when it came to me and the kids and grandkids. So, to blaze the trail to heaven first—yes, I could expect that and accept that from Steve. I felt he was telling me today not to be scared or concerned. Most importantly, not to dwell on it. So, I haven't. I have lights everywhere. Lights make me happy. Really, they make everyone happy. It's why we look forward to the Christmas season. Beautiful lights give us the spark for the holiday spirit, for peace and joy, for thankfulness and love. It is also a reflective time for everyone, because some of our best memories revolve around Christmastime. I hope you hang some lights soon, lots of lights, and above all, please make some really, *really* good memories.

This keeps me afloat:

My hope is built on nothing less

Than Jesus Christ, my righteousness.

I dare not trust the sweetest frame

But wholly lean on Jesus's name.

On Christ, the solid Rock, I stand.

All other ground is sinking sand.

All other ground is sinking sand. ("My Hope Is Built on Nothing Less"; lyrics by Edward Mote)

I know I post on Facebook a lot, and most of it is totally unnecessary. But my feelings are deep and passionate about everything, and I am alone. When the thoughts cannot be contained, I write. My heart is full tonight. I think the most beautiful thing God gave us is love. Wow. Who could ever explain it? You will have to feel it to know it. Even knowing it does not mean you will ever be able to fully explain it. It is a mystery how it happens. I remember one time when Steve was very sick with the cancer and I had made him a bed on the couch in the den. Whenever he got up to go to the bathroom, I would straighten his covers, smooth out the sheets, and get the blanket positioned just right for him to slide in, and then I would cover him up. One day when he was returning to the bed, he knew I had been doing this straightening thing every time, so he said, "Why do you love me so much?" I truly could not find the words. My heart was so full of love for him, and hundreds of things streamed across my mind of how good and loving he had always been. How he had provided for me and the kids. How love had flourished between two kids and kindled a lifetime of respect, loyalty, and devotion. I knew he had always known all of that because we had always told each other these things. So, I just whispered, "Because I love you so, and because I know you would do the very same for me." I think at that moment it became very clear to me what real love is. It is sacrificing your deepest emotions, your deepest being for someone else. It is the desire to even take their place, if you could, to spare them what they are experiencing. I know I am learning. It is baby steps in this new life that I did not choose or want. I am determined to make it through, even though it is so very painful at times. But that is when I must write. I don't have to share, but I need to. I need to tell you, because you all are becoming my best friends and I love you.

I want people to understand that you can have the pinnacle of faith, but you don't always get the things you desperately want. That is when true faith must take over. You must believe that God has ordained and appropriated certain things that will hurt deeply. My advice to you is this—just as I felt at that time and still do. Where else can you go when you face the unpleasant, hurtful, devastating things? There is nowhere else to go but to your God, the great I Am. And if you do not get what you ask for, well, please believe that it is not because you do not have enough faith. Never let anyone tell you that. You must place your faith, without conditions, in the Lord's hands, and then hold on. If you want to, you can ask Him later, when you are face-to-face, "Why?" But here on earth, just understand that sometimes there will be no answer to why. I know for a fact that you will change and that your faith in Him will become stronger when you acknowledge that He controls all things and that He knows what is up ahead on your journey.

There are a million thoughts in my head since last night. When tossing and turning gets to be like a workout, that is when I know it is just better to get up. In the stillness of an early morning, and especially as I hear the low rumble of thunder and the sound of rain, my mind goes back and forth from past to present. From days when I was a child and Daddy and Mama were my world. Sometimes it drifts to high school, where I was so divinely happy with so many good times and people and fun. A blooming time for me, where I felt my worth surrounded by people I absolutely loved, and they loved me. Visions of a better time, or so it seemed in those days. I am sure it was the hopefulness of youth and the exuberance of coming upon the cusp of being an adult. Little did we know what all that would mean. Thoughts of a wild-spirited young man who captured my heart with his craziness, boldness, sense of humor, and love. What a magnificent ride he took me on. Not one day of regret do I have. Two babies that were a joy and have filled me with such pride. They were my completion, my heart, my world. I cannot believe all the life in between that I have lived, such sweet times, scary times, growing times, hard times, and sad times. Looking back, I feel like I should have already been approaching Methuselah's age, and sometimes I hope I can. My thoughts of the present are light again. I have found that we are our own worst enemies most of the time. When life changes drastically, and not in a good way, it is hard to look beyond the moment, the pain, and the disbelief. In this life, I have learned that a "herd" of friends is perhaps the most valuable thing you can acquire here on earth. They become your saviors many times. I thought about every single friend I have this morning, from California to North Carolina, from Tennessee to Louisiana, from Minnesota to Georgia, from Colorado to Utah, from Idaho to Oklahoma, and from Texas to Israel. I could see the faces from coast to coast and beyond. How very grateful I am for this life filled with hope and love by way of others in my life. Today is Friday, and it had always been my happiest day. But for a while, the threshold of the weekend was a bit cloudy and gray. God was preparing me, letting me heal properly, teaching me, holding me together, and strengthening me for now. I have learned you must never say never to an ever-changing world and life. You must always be open to God's plan for your life and the fact you could be His plan for someone else's life. I don't profess to understand this life or its ups and downs, its complications and disappointments, its twists and turns. I only know that we are born to live it, and what a privilege that is. I preach all the time not to waste a minute. Do things, love life and people, take the good with the bad, and always have faith. Believe even when you don't see a way. Don't be so hard on yourself. We are all flawed but worthy and loved by the One who knows us best. When I feel I am not good enough, I always think of King David, who wrote the book of Psalms in the Holy Bible. He was so very flawed. He committed many sins that are well documented. He failed God many times over, yet God loved him, forgave him, and brought His very own Son out of David's lineage. Hope, belief, trust, faith, and love are life. So today I continue to move forward because that is where the Lord is taking me. Please, my friends, journey with me.

I don't know if this will help anyone, but I want to post it. It has helped me many times. Steve was in Vietnam in 1967–1968. He saw a lot of things that he could not unsee or unknow. He was a remarkable guy with the most positive attitude. He told me that the only way he could ever get through what he saw and experienced in the Vietnam War was his belief that God, the Creator, knows the number of days that we will be here the moment we are conceived. It has been predetermined by Him. Steve reasoned that no matter where the boys he saw die were, their days were over at their appointed time. He felt the same way about his own life and his own time to leave here. It was his appointed time. When I can just hardly bear the sadness, I try to remember that. But as a human, it does not keep me from being disappointed that God did not appropriate more time for him. He was a solid rock, genuine, one-of-a-kind guy. But I also know that God wants and needs just that kind of a man back at some point. I will always struggle with not having him to continue our journey together, but I do know that he is good now, well now, and happy. I want to live life full out, joyfully like he wanted me to, just doing anything I can to help others until my appointed time. These are the thoughts that get me through. I hope this helps someone who is struggling to make any sense out of their loss.

The words in my heart today: I am so glad that I trusted the Lord to direct my earthly love; I will be blessed forevermore. The happiest people are those not afraid to give their love away. I had that. I had one who gave me all his love, and what a remarkable love it was.

Okay, tell me how strange this is. I was at a clothing store today, and as I was looking over the merchandise, I heard songs from Michael Bublé, Keith Urban, One Direction, and Ariana Grande. Then suddenly this song came on: "Homesick" by Mercy Me. That was one of the songs played at Steve's memorial service. It's about someone really loved being in heaven and the ones left here to mourn and how they feel. They are homesick for heaven and wanting to be with the one they have lost. I have never heard that song played in a clothing store before, and the timing? Wow! To be played when I was there? Coincidence? I don't think so. Meaning? Not sure. Did Steve want me to know he was around me and with me? I am telling you this has been a difficult week so far for mourning. Not sure if the message was from Steve or God or both. I left in a daze. Remarkable. Just remarkable.

I miss the old hymns. I miss church. I will get back there, hopefully soon. I am getting there slowly. Tried to go back in the beginning, but when the hymns started, so did my tears. God is good. He told me that He's right there with me wherever I am, and He will be there with me at church when I am ready. He is patient and kind and loving. He is my Best Friend.

Everything is so much brighter when the sun shines. Thank You, Lord. FYI, He is the guy who is taking care of me now. Some days He just lets me wander around until I realize I cannot do it or get through it without Him. Then He reels me back in, and I know where I am going and who I am really following.

On Saturday nights, I always have the best intentions to arise on Sunday morning, get dressed, and get to church. I have only been able to do this sporadically, which lays the guilt on this Texas, Southern Baptist girl. I am not mad at God, although being honest, I must admit I am disappointed that we did not get the healing or outcome we wanted on this side. I am pretty private about showing my grief. Steve and I did everything together, and church was one of those things. We are not fanatical or there every time the doors were open, but we shared a love for the Lord very much alike. I do pray, and I thank the Lord for the opportunity of being Steve's wife for so many years. We grew up together and experienced so much together. I am especially thankful to Him for allowing me to experience the true love of a good man. I know He understands my absence from the church pew on Sunday morning and am sure He will continue to hold my seat, knowing I need just a little more time to sort things out.

Sometimes reality just throws you a punch so you can learn and feel something. That happened to me today. A friend lost her husband a short time ago, and now she has lost a son. I say that is a description of unspeakable sadness and unbearable pain. Knowing this friend, I have no doubt she will continue through the darkness until the Lord leads her into the sunlight. All the while, He will be whispering to her, "They are safe and free and with me forevermore, and in a little while, you will see them again." The wider your circle of friends, the more your soul is touched, and your heartfelt love can be released. The greatest feeling though is to feel so deeply for friends in these painful times. And then when it is your turn, there they are with open arms and kind and gentle words and beautiful prayers to get you through.

There is something empowering yet humbling about the full moon in the country sky. You feel quiet and peaceful and reverent in its presence. No lights or city noise to ruin the moment. It is just you, the glowing nightlight, and a sprinkling of stars in the distant heavens. With your full attention, in this setting, God speaks His sweetest words of love to you.

So, I am melancholy tonight. I swear it is the caffeine in the morning that propels me into manic posting on Facebook. Then later, like now, I just feel like I fell off a cliff. Even out, girl! You have a bit of living to do! When I look back, I do not know how I did it. I coordinated so much stuff to care for Steve. I scheduled so much that it makes my head spin to think about it now. I ramrodded conventional and unconventional treatments and talked to numerous doctors and medical personnel. I took him to all his appointments. I took care of his food diet, his liquid intake, and his medications. I took care of making him comfortable in every way possible. I dealt with my own spiritual ups and downs. I continued to take care of my mother who was ninety-two years old. I dealt with the loss of my father at age ninety. I took care of all our finances. I took care of the maintenance for the house and the yard. Good grief! I know God saw all of that and gave me strength to accomplish it. I know that I was a good wife. He always told me that, and I know, without a doubt, he would have done the same for me.

It was another day, and she was thinking out loud. "How many sunrises have I seen?" She smiled as she answered herself, "Not enough!"

The days disappear too quickly in the hubbub of life. Slow down! Each day, though it may seem ordinary, is a different page in your book of life. And just as you are, it is unique, never to come around in the same way again. Days, even ordinary days, are opportunities. Opportunities to do good, to discover, to appreciate, to live, to be thankful, and to praise.

Each sunrise is a miracle, and so are you.

THE RAINBOW

When you come out of the storm's tunnel, you will begin to yearn to find some lasting peace. For me, it took a while to understand that I was an individual now and not a couple anymore. The lyrics to Stevie Nicks' song "Landslide" did so resonate with me. Especially these words:

> Can the child within my heart rise above? Can I sail through the changin' ocean tides? Can I handle the seasons of my life? Well, I've been 'fraid of changin' cause, I've built my life around you. But time makes you bolder. Even children get older. And I'm getting older too.

Nowhere is it written how to proceed after such a personal loss as a spouse. You see, we are all different and unique, not carbon copies. I realized I would have PTSD the rest of my life. I would never be free to enjoy certain songs, scents, places, things, or people without pain in my heart and many times a lump in my throat and tears streaming down my cheeks. I have written to ease my burdened heart and to release my emotions. Also, to be there with my words for anyone who endures a similar personal loss so deep. I want you to know you will be okay. You will change, but you will survive. The wound it leaves will always be tender, never completely to heal. Striving to continue and to find out who you are is confusing at times. Some people will judge you. They will assess that you should be this way or that way according to their own ideas. Please don't listen. Talk to God and pray earnestly for wisdom, knowledge, direction, purpose, and peace. There will be a day when you realize the rainbow you need after the storm is *yourself.*

It may be scary at first, but the more you discover who you are, and who God wants you to be, then you will become bolder in your decisions and know when they are what you want, but more importantly, what you need.

Life will always be a challenge, whether you remain by yourself or choose to be with someone else. I am a firm believer in counseling with the Lord about every decision that may come your way. His voice is within you. It is in your spirit. You will know when you have taken the right path. It will flow. There will not be so many starts and stops that you are filled with frustration or angst. Believe me: it will not always be easy just because you are counseling with the Lord, but you will become more aware of His leading. Failures only mean lessons to the committed believer. There is not one thing that touches a child of God that is not for a purpose, regardless of what it is. Most importantly, every experience here on earth is training for a heavenly purpose. I like to think of it as vocational training for our future in eternity. Just as we are all different here with different strengths and talents, so I believe it will be in heaven. Please continue to pursue who you were created to be. Please continue to pursue happiness and peace. Please continue to pursue the Lord Jesus Christ. On that one, I know we can never out love Him.

Misunderstandings, misspoken words, broken hearts, doubts, fears, and loneliness. Just like the raging storms of nature, nothing remains the same forever. God clears the heart and mind, just like He clears the storm clouds and places a rainbow in the sky. Nothing remains the same forever.

I have found at the bottom of sadness that the heart will always hope. I have discovered that I have many facets, many components to me. Rebuilding happiness is also rebuilding me. I am not the same person that I have been for so long a time. I am the slightly different person that God has enabled me and instructed me to become. I have chosen to not let grief kill me and not to let loss define me. I have chosen to make changes, which to some are painful but to me have been my salvation. When there is much life to be lived, it cannot be lived secluded and always sad, always in mourning. It takes time for scar tissue to form over a deep wound of the body and of the soul. It takes time for the heart and mind to process a great personal loss. How long? It will vary according to the person, the loss, and God's will. I am not an authority on life after loss. I am just a traveler in this world who had to take a new path, a new direction, new goals, and exercise new thinking. God has been extremely good to me. He has been holding me up for a long time now. He has been gently loving me until I was ready to progress forward. To get to the progress was painful at times, but just to be progressing is monumental.

To be living again is the best feeling in the whole world. God has blessed me with an extraordinary person in my life again. He is restoring all those things that I had lost. Knowing that God had the guiding hand in this just makes it all that much sweeter. When I see the beautiful moon, I still think of the deep meaning it has to me. My love has moved way past the beautiful full moon. There is so much happiness in heaven. All its inhabitants want only what is best for us who are still here on planet earth, living and striving to finish the race. I have come to a place finally where there is peace in my heart, joy in my spirit, and an easiness in my soul. I am different, but I am good. Life is different, but it is still very, very, good.

Newness, beginnings, changes, choices, and survival—you will find yourself at the threshold of each of these doors in your lifetime. Be sure you know the One who holds all the keys.

I just don't want to be sad anymore. Sad says you are stuck in one miserable place. It is the tsunami of disparaging emotions. We were not created to be that way. I want to soar with happiness. And even though some sad things tag along, I will not let them drag me back to an unchangeable place I do not want to be. Rise and walk. Some of the sweetest words from our Lord to a man caught in lameness and sadness. I take those words to say to anyone caught in life's sadness and troubles to rise above and walk forward, with Him, one foot in front of the other.

It felt strange to be this new person, this individual she had been struggling to find since he had been taken away. What she discovered was that she was strong. She was brave. She could do anything she set her mind to. Her negative thoughts had been altered by prayers to a loving God. He steered her forward to a new future with aspirations and desires. Her strength had been nurtured by her friends. They had been as attentive as mother hens and as protective as shields of steel, never letting her fall into that deep, depressing pit of despair that she had inched toward in the beginning. They taught her to have hope and to still believe in life and purpose. They encouraged her to continue to dream and pursue happiness however she desired. It had taken time to evolve, to want to come out of the cocoon. She knew there would still be days that weren't so good. The ones where the memories come flooding in. It might be a song or a scent, just a certain way the sun was shining, or the way the moon was full, surrounded by a billion stars on a summer night, but she was prepared. She would embrace the memories, for they were part of what propelled her to where she was now and who she was now. The old and the new combined into one soul. She was beginning to feel her worth again. Her longings had been quieted, and now her spirit was ready to soar.

I will live in this day, for I know sometimes tomorrows never come. I will love in this day, for I know the importance of expressing feelings at the very moment they are felt, because that moment may never come again. I will be grateful on this day for the richness of God's blessings of life and love and pray that from His bounty, He will grant me more.

Just get up every day and do what is necessary. Sometimes the weeks will surprise you. Sometimes nothing happens, or it seems. But I like to believe that He is preparing some of the best chapters in my life to begin at any moment.

I think upon my life and all the events and happenings, all the people, souls, and spirits that I have touched and that have touched me, and I feel a deepness, an awareness of how utterly magnificent life is. Yet how complicated we make it sometimes. We hold our breath, we dread, and we forget to live in the present. Either thinking too much about the past or worrying about the future. We forget that our lives are ordained from heaven and the steps we trod today are more important than any other. For our lives are as running streams headed to the mouth of a vast ocean. The flow of our lives touches only that moment, that very moment. Life and death, war and peace, joy and pain, love and loss, and the warmth and the bitter cold of feelings are but seasons to our lives. All that touches us, teaches us, and has purpose and meaning. The world's direction, no matter the winds of today, are for heaven's purposes, and so are we. We live the seasons of our lives best and easier knowing their ebb and flow are orchestrated from above.

Be worthy of someone who gives you their heart. Love and loyalty should not be separated. There is no better aphrodisiac than all-consuming faithfulness. The proof of real love.

Be thankful for the beautiful mornings. Thankfulness gives hope, and hope gives life to your spirit. A renewed spirit gives life meaning, meaning gives opportunity for purpose, purpose gives joy, joy gives love, and love gives thankfulness.

Just take life wherever it leads you, to the valley or the mountaintop. You won't stay at either place forever, so enjoy the highs and know you need to gather strength and determination and courage for the lows that surely will come to block your path. Even in the midst of the most grueling trial, remember that each day holds promises that may be just what you needed. So, don't give up! To give up is to give in, to give in is to settle, and to settle means it's not what you need or want or where you wish to be. When you are in the valley, then float. Float your thoughts to pleasant things and places, never engaging too deeply in fret or worry about the valley you find yourself in. Float until you have floated up, up, up to a mountain peak again. Savor your joy no matter how momentary it may be. For it is the gathering and the remembering of simple joys that will keep you rising. Just as life is always moving and changing, so we must learn to do the same.

Life cannot always be perfect, but it can be good. Life cannot always be happy, but it can be worthwhile. There is a meaning and a lesson to every day you live. Some lessons will be for you, and some will be for others. Gaining knowledge about life is sometimes painful, yet the lessons learned by pain are the ones we retain the longest and the best. And if we choose, they are the ones that make us stronger, kinder, and more compassionate.

Don't know what it is about Mondays that makes me want to write, but I always seem to be full of emotions and words after the weekends. If you are a writer, artist, or musician, you understand the feeling. The urges don't die until you release the words or the paint or the music. I marvel at those who can paint or draw, capturing the eye's image so well and transferring that along with their own emotions onto canvas or paper. And the music, so personal to the composer, poetry from the heart. To anyone who shares their gift, whether it be writing, music, or visual art, it is a cathartic event that must happen in order to clear the mind and get some peace. My emotions have been high of late. So much of life comes all at once and when we least expect it. Or how we expect it. I have taken many steps in the last two years. I had no map. My journey has been uncharted. I have written to encourage any new travelers on a similar path that they neither expected nor wanted. One of the most important parts of my new road has been discovering who I am and defining my own feelings. When you have been a wife and a mom for a long time, you know who you are, where you belong, and what to do. But when you are no longer a wife but a widow, you become confused, caught between what was and what is. It is a real struggle that can wear you out and wear you down. Time is your helper, but you won't feel that way at first. It takes months into your new journey to settle down and to find some moments of calmness.

There will be endless restless thoughts of the past to pull you off your path and delay your progress. There will countless moments of feeling lost and detached, even from your children and friends. My loving advice to you is to keep your blinders on. Resist too much time thinking of what was. The past has a way of pulling you under. Try to reserve the memories for a time when you have marked enough days progressing miles and miles ahead, and after you have found a new purpose or a new strength in yourself. You may feel battered at times, but you have to put one foot in front of the other, moving ahead, even if it is at a snail's pace. Anything you experience or feel is okay. There are no guidelines or rulebooks for recovering or discovering your life after loss. I do know this: just as I was encouraged by some others who had begun their new life's journey ahead of me, the days will get easier and the nights will not be as painful. The thoughts of the past will not frequent you as violently as in the beginning. Remember that you are designed for a purpose that is all your own. I hope you are a believer, because the One who created you is the Mapmaker of your own personal journey and destination. He has a towing service twenty-four hours a day, seven days a week, to pull you out of the dumps or charge your battery to get you moving forward, and He is an expert in damage control repairing any dents in your psyche. He is a Master at painting your future a beautiful new color with hope, love, and purpose.

I am not in charge of my life, and I never want to be. I would surely make it a big, fat mess. When I feel myself holding on too tightly to anything or trying to control it, I back away and give it to the One who has a better understanding of me, my life, my future, what I need, and where I need to be. Not an easy thing to do, and the learning and implementing of this is not easy either. Facing and living with something you cannot control humbles you, frightens you, angers you, and saddens you. When you work through all of that, then you will give the uncontrollable to Him. You will struggle at times trying to take it back. But the things of this world, with no understanding, warning, or solution to be found, need to be laid in His hands daily. Minute to minute if need be. That doesn't mean everything will work out or be answered. It just means you have trusted the only One who knows your unknown, the world's unknowns, and can lead you gently through.

She felt alone a lot of the time. She wasn't, but there was always this sense of isolation within. No one really understood her feelings and her darkness at times, not even her. She kept waiting for this epiphany, this divine revelation, for direction, meaning, and purpose. She was not hopeless, for she had been delivered from herself and her deep internal struggles before. She held on only by faith. Even if it was by one single fragile thread. That fragile thread was reinforced from somewhere. She chose to believe that it was the One, True, Living God that held her in the balance and that He would never let her fall. She was different. She was complicated, yet her heart was open, always seeking the closeness and understanding that seemed to elude her.

My heart is passionate. I feel things deeply until they hurt, but the pain is worth it. It is freedom because it means I am alive. I care. I am honest with myself and to anyone or to anything I have passion for. When I leave this world, I will have left every drop of care, love, myself, and the beautiful passion that God has given me.

My heart is so full today that the overflow has been leaking from my eyes. Sometimes in a painful part of your journey, you can encounter something that invades your heart and mind and changes your direction, the course you are on, and your way of thinking. Never try to understand life. It is best enjoyed in the freedom of not trying too hard or thinking too deeply. Take advantage of what God puts in front of you. Today, I am feeling a different kind of happiness that I welcome and like a lot. Maybe at this crossroads, I have taken the right path.

Now is the time to celebrate. Now is the time to be happy. Embrace today as if it were the ticket to your dreams. I watched the clock one day, and as the second hand moved ever so quickly, I thought, *Those tiny fleeting seconds are gone forever, never to be back.* It was the past forming before my very eyes. It propelled my thinking as to how brief life really is upon planet Earth and how important every second is. Do not slight any second of time, my friends, because they are all valuable. If there is no work to be done or decisions to be made, then dwell upon good thoughts of past and present. Dream of things that make you happy. Mark your time with pleasing accomplishments and worthwhile ventures. Above all, let the second of your life reflect joy, peace, and love.

When your life has a big change, change with it. You can no longer be who you were. The only things that need to stay the same are your values, your core. The most surprising thing you will discover is *not* that people are not what you thought they were but that *you* are not what you thought you were. It is not a bad thing; it is just a difference, a newness that you must embrace, accept, build on, and learn. I heard this yesterday: "Life is just a series of problems that you have to solve, one after another, until you die." I must add to this that if, at the solving of these problems, you never learn anything or grow from the results, or share the knowledge of the experience, then you have truly missed the meaning of life.

I have found out many things about life, including that you can be at your happiest and it can change in an instant. That you can find the strength within to do the hardest things you will ever encounter. That you get your courage from God and friends. That you will only have one mother and one father, and you need to savor time with them. That when your world is shattered, the world and life keep on going even if you do not want them to. That not everyone understands the changes you must make in order to survive and continue to live. That being hopeful, optimistic, and prayerful are the only ways to tackle the world. That a mother holds many hurts and wrongs in her heart but continues to love with no reservations. That time moves faster as you get older. That memories and tender moments are golden. That if you let the Lord lead, you will never get lost. That if you try to understand the world, you only get more confused. That if you pursue your passion, you feel contentment. That helping others can be addictive and keeps your spirit healthy. That God is the only One who knows what is best for you, and if you believe that, He will get you there. That patience is the hardest thing to master. That real and lasting joy is found in your children and grandchildren. And above all, that God has always and will always be in control of all things and truthfully will love you, understand you, and be there, even when you cannot feel Him.

No matter what you are facing—loss, imminent loss, heartache of any kind, fear, rejection, or personal crisis—I know this to be absolute truth. Christ has been my steady Friend, never leaving my side through my entire up and down life. Really, that is all that matters now or in the end. I am acknowledging His genuine and ever-abiding love for me and for you.

....your kingdom come, your will be done on earth as it is in heaven. (Matthew 6:10 NIV)

There is a lot said in that short verse, which is the ending of our Lord's instructions on how to pray. I know the older you get, the more your eyes are opened to the world. That on the one hand, while you enjoy the world for the most part, you realize there must be so much more. Something so much better. I know that is when your eyes begin to look increasingly more often for the promised kingdom to come. The earth is a constant war zone with seen and unseen battles taking place. Some days, it is as if you are a soldier fighting for your very survival, physically, emotionally, and spiritually. That is where the words "Your will be done" must take over. I do think that is the hardest prayer to pray in the beginning, because we are accustomed to handling things ourselves. We figure and decide our own paths, drawing our own conclusions and then committing them. There will times though when all your decisions are not working. Your best-laid plans are failing, and there does not seem to be a path you can find for resolution and restored calm. When you get to that point, you are ready to pray those words in earnest. Even amid the scariest of turmoil, you are at the beginning of practicing the wisdom our Lord was instructing us to use in His guiding prayer. Scary at first, but it becomes liberating. When you have worked the problem with everything humanly possible, and there is no answer, then it is God's turn. I am not saying the answer or solution will be immediate, but the One who knows the answer will be in charge. Your work will now be patience, trust, and faith. As the ending of the Lord's prayer informs us, "On earth as it is in heaven," you must realize that allowing and practicing God's will be done here on earth now is really training for eternity. I have had many storms the last six years. I know from personal experience the more you pray and mean the words "Your will be done," the freer and more content you become. The pressure is not yours. I look for God's solutions every day. Truly, that is what keeps me getting up. God's way in God's time, the key to surviving life.

So, bring me tomorrow and all the hope and joy of a new day, for I have been sad for too long. I have cried a million tears. My heart has ached with no solace. I could not see beyond the clouds. But in tomorrow, there is a chance, an opportunity for changes and beginnings. A glimpse of sunlight and warmth to heal my heart and set my spirit free.

Choose the path you want. Love honestly. Live passionately. Be happy. Be joyful. Be thankful. Be kind. Walk in the sunshine. Dream in the moonlight and dare to believe those dreams will come true.

Take time for your mourning, but you owe your Creator the respect and gratefulness to let Him do with your life and living what He designed you for as an individual and as a unique miracle creation of the Most High God.

And now these three remain: faith, hope, and love. But the greatest of these is love. (1 Corinthians 13:13 NIV)

I truly understand this scripture to the fullest lately. Faith and hope are definitely needed on this earth because we have no knowledge of the future and we cling to the promises of what is to come as believers. But when we arrive in heaven, our faith and hope are fulfilled. But love is eternal. There is no end, whether here on earth or in heaven. God Himself has no need of faith or hope because He is the fulfillment of those, but He has designed Himself to not only be Perfect Love but to need love too from us. The need, fulfillment, satisfaction, joy, euphoria, strength, confidence, encouragement, security, and truth are all in love. We all crave it. As the apostle Paul so wisely wrote these words down, the simplicity of deep meaning is there for all to read and comprehend. These three remain: faith, hope and love. But the greatest of these is love.

Sometime the truth shows up like a golden supermoon. You cannot miss it. It fills your mind as clearly and brightly as those moonbeams do fill the ebony sky.

There have been days that were bleak, dark, cold, and sad, yet I went on. Not really meaning to, but kept afloat by the Power that designed me, owned me, and loved me. In all those days, the life I was living was meaningful, even though at times, I could see no purpose. I have learned that there will be periods of nothing that make sense and days of longing for normalcy. I am not sure why or how I came through the darkness. I can only believe that just as the moonlight illuminates a dark path at night, there was a hidden light before me that only my spirit could see. It drew me forward inch by inch until time put enough distance between me and the pain. I feel the sunshine now. I believe in going on. I believe in new life, purpose, happiness, dreams, and love. If there is one thing that I can convey to any disheartened soul who is weary of the fight, weary of the loneliness, and weary of how slowly life drags on in your heartache, it is to hold on. Never think too deeply. Wait for your spirit to find the light to lead you out of the night, and grab hold of it tightly. Believe that there is life to be lived, purposes to be fulfilled, and happiness waiting.

What is Faith? It is the confident assurance that something we want is going to happen. It is the certainty that what we hope for is waiting for us, even though we cannot see it up ahead. (Hebrews 11:1 TLB) Just believe that. Your relief is before you, waiting for you to arrive.

I've been thinking tonight, as we approach Valentine's Day, just how special love is. Do you remember when you were an early teen and, in the blink of an eye, the opposite sex became something quite different from boring, obnoxious, and covered with cooties? Wasn't that a glorious feeling? I was just thinking about God creating that need and want and emotion in all of us. How gracious that was. That part of our design that causes us to want and to share this love with someone. You must admit that if you have found it and given yours to the right person, there is no greater feeling, fulfillment, or completeness. The heart is a complicated thing. When it decides on someone, there is no changing it. It seems no matter what happens, the heart rules us. I know the heart can convince the brain of things that the brain could never convince the heart to believe. The heart knows love. It knows us deeply to the core. It is the center of our feelings and emotions. It is that part of our Creator that He so graciously decided to gift to each human being, so that we could experience this wonderful thing called love in so many forms. It is the designated season to express your love for that special person. Listen to your heart. Express it with reckless abandon. Do it while you can.

Home is where you feel loved and comfortable. Where you feel safe, understood, and wanted. The heart wants what it wants, and it longs to feel at home. When you find your home, never leave or let it go.

And when you have earnestly prayed, trust the decisions that you make. Do not look back or around or fret or second-guess. Move forward with the confidence that the Lord is holding the lamp, leading you from your darkness.

Deciding to move forward is a decision the spirit makes. It does not mean you forget or lose your past, your memories, or your love. It means the will of the heart to continue to beat is made. The eyes must look ahead more often. The need to laugh is craved more than the tears, so resilience is spawned. Deciding to move forward means never choose stagnation with anything or anyone. If it does not flow and if it doesn't progress, leave it behind. Losing the most important thing in life will propel you to deeply understand the meaning of true love and true living. From the depths of pain, knowledge and courage are learned and retained. Life is to be lived. Move forward. Always move forward.

God knows what He has planned for every life given to Him. When He destines certain things, they can be surprising but never doubted. Hope springs eternal in the hearts of those who love and acknowledge the Lord.

When you have no other choice, let go.

When you don't know what to do, just "float."

When you feel a calling, answer it.

When things feel right, do them.

When your thoughts are muddled, quit thinking.

When your heart hurts, pray.

When happiness appears, choose it.

When life changes, embrace it.

There will be times in your life when you must retreat inward. Alone time with yourself is one of the keys to survival in difficult times, in confusing times, in times of self-doubt, or in crazy times that the world offers up on occasion. I have found that thinking, reasoning, and trusting your own mind can save you from speaking too soon, speaking too much, or causing yourself more grief in certain situations. I am an inward person by nature. That is why I write. I believe it is important to take those moments of quiet, inward thoughts as often as possible. It is amazing to me how many times I have talked myself through some difficult times, problematic times, and just, plain awkward times by simply thinking. Never saying a single word aloud.

Sometimes you must endure some things silently, never uttering your feelings, pains, doubts, or fears. Thoughts and feelings that we share with and confess to only ourselves are the very essence of who we are. They are our core, our soul, and our truth. There is no pretense when we address ourselves. We already know who we are. The key to being whole is to know yourself well, to like yourself, and to trust yourself. Not everything needs to be shared with others or the world. Contentment can come with learning to tuck away in the heart some thoughts of life that are so personal, so special that they become treasures for us alone.

Ebb and Flow: a recurrent or rhythmical pattern of coming and going or decline and regrowth.

And that is life. Just like the waves of the ocean. Our being is constantly moving or subsiding, growing, or shrinking. Always responding to and dependent on the pull of forces in our life and of the world. If we never had the ebbing of life, we would never learn or feel the great joy that smooth sailing brings. We must be reminded when we view the beauty and wonder of the ocean that it truly represents life. Its course was set from the beginning of time. It will have ebbs and flows for as long as it is here, and there is a vast force much greater than circumstances, luck, or fate that forms its purpose for being. It does not fight against the force that drives it but takes the pulling of the tides with constant endurance. It is no wonder that we feel such awe when we look upon the ocean. We are akin to it, and like the ebb and flow of the waves in the vast waters, we live the same way in the vastness of life.

Go for it! Whatever you want. Never think too much or too deeply about it. My husband was my mentor on this subject. He had confidence and truth that was so admirable. He never knew the word *can't*. He always told me, "No one cares more about you and your life than *you*." You'd better do it. Take a chance. Take a leap. If it doesn't work like you expected, at least you'll know. Shake off the dust and move forward. Leave no stone unturned, and never be intimidated. Strength is found in confidence, and confidence is found in trying. Lessons in life come from trying, whether winning comes or not. It is the effort that gains us the knowledge until a victory we crave comes.

In the mornings, my mind is like a menagerie.

People, things, thoughts. Who I was and want to be.

Sometimes I feel a weight so heavy and strong,

And other times, I awake listening to a dove's song.

The strides of one's life can be laboriously long,

With twists and turns, some right and some wrong.

Who can rightfully judge the thoughts in my head

Or know the pain and fear and doubts I am fed

By a world of people who have not a clue

Of how I have fought and wept and finally grew

To be this person standing in morning's light

Just a little bruised and scarred from my fight

To reach a place that feels okay

To stop and rest and possibly stay

We all must wage some battles in life

And trudge through failures, regrets, and strife.

But this is what I have come to believe:

Trust your heart, yourself in this journey you weave,

For on this earth, there is nary a one

Who truly knows the distance you've come.

So, when the menagerie of thoughts begin,

I tell myself, "I know where I have been.

It is not the place God intended me to stay.

I am moving forward. Get out of my way."

I've been in deep thoughts this week. I became another year older. I decided to take a chance and make a move. It takes courage to try to find your new way and make changes after you lose someone you had planned on being with until you were one hundred. Maybe it just takes being a little bit crazy. I know that life is brief. You blink and your routine wonderful life is over. It really has never taken a lot to make me happy. Being loved, being with friends, being with family, laughing, and trying to be the best I can be. Sometimes I am not sure what the right way is to go or how things will work out from here. Chances are risks, and I guess that's what we do every day we step out our front door. So, I will be stepping out my front door soon, taking the biggest chance of my life.

To know when something or someone is right for you, you must first really know yourself, like yourself, and feel that you deserve the best. When there is an ease to a situation or relationship, that is a clue that you may be headed in the right direction. If it doesn't flow, let it go. Prayer is essential. If God knows you care enough to consult with Him over relationships, opportunities, or situations, I guarantee He will heighten your commonsense and allow you to make the right decisions eventually. Don't ignore what you feel. That gut instinct is your commonsense speaking. Life is so full of goodness, yet there are pitfalls and land mines scattered along the way. Not every wrong turn is a disaster. It may just be knowledge wrapped in momentary disappointment or temporary failure. Head up, forward march, no looking or turning back. Be willing to change or take a chance. Just believe that your life came with good plans and the means to get there. Embrace all the time God gives you and use it wisely. Be thankful for the knowledge you gain in life, no matter how it comes, and use it to help yourself and others. Clean slate starts tomorrow. Unfold some beautiful chapters to your life story.

I am packing today for a move to East Texas. I am still amazed at how life can change in an instant, good or bad. I never thought that I could find something a second time in my life that was genuinely good and real. Some people don't want or need that again, and that's okay. We are all different. Some of us so thoroughly enjoyed making someone else happy and being loved that life is just empty without it. Children and grandchildren and friends fill part of the void, but there is something programmed in some that keeps life feeling incomplete without that someone special. I make no apologies for being the latter. I am designed by God for specific purposes that even I do not know. But I do know this: I have heard Him whisper to me in my darkest moments when I have felt that my heart was bleeding. He let me know that I am His, and He knows me and loves me and has plans that continue, even though my Steve is gone. I think He may have been speaking through Steve when, on our most serious talk of all, Steve encouraged me to enjoy life to the fullest. He said life is not to be wasted. I loved his words to me. Very private, but I have shared some because I want anyone going through the devastation of losing a love that you thought would be there forever to understand. Life as a widow or widower is for living the way you choose to continue and to heal. You owe no one else any explanation. We are who we have been created to be. It is best to understand and know yourself first and get plenty of healing days in. Life is short. When the life you want comes along, take it, settle in, and live it. God can teach us much in quiet, alone time with Him, especially when we seek His advice and guidance.

I have had a terrible storm in my life for so long that it is hard for me to accept or believe that I can be happy again. My past happiness and love are eternal, frozen in time, and never to be forgotten. But sometimes things happen, signs appear, and God works in a way that you must acknowledge He has had a hand in some new happiness coming into your life. I do not believe in coincidence or luck. I believe in God putting things together, making a plan, showing you those signs, and having you discover new happiness. I have discovered that, and it feels so good and so right, like moonlight on the water, my life is glistening again.

I believe in hoping for good things.

I believe in praying for good things.

I believe when I am given good things,

It is because God heard me hoping and praying for good things.

There is not one thing that touches my life

That He has not ordained or allowed—the good, the bad, and the ugly.

When I was on my knees in prayer on my worst days,

I felt His sadness

As He heard me plead for something that He knew He could not give.

Yet I loved Him so in-spite of my disappointment.

I continue to believe in hoping for good things.

I continue to pray for good things.

I continue to believe that He hears me hoping and praying for good things.

I wait upon my Lord.

And I love Him so.

I was sad for a long time,

Not really knowing who I am anymore

Or even how to act or what to say.

Life had brought changes that I had not wanted,

The kind that are treacherous and can only

Be overcome with supernatural strength and faith.

I emerged a different person,

Seeking happiness and newness.

My life before and the sadness had melded

Together, making me a different being.

Some did not understand who I was now,

But they were not there in the dark

When my heart was breaking

And the tears would not stop,

So, I emerged from that darkness

With a new spirit and optimism that would not dim.

Future: Still to come.

I am so glad to be thinking about a future with things to come. I had no clue a short time ago about any future or anything in this life to give me that light that drives one forward. I was stuck between the ugly face of death and existing with its lack of hope and enthusiasm. I have learned that one needs friends and family to convince them to hold on while the life you are meant to have catches you. I have heard from so many people since I started writing about this part of my journey. Some to thank me for my words and to say that the words have helped them to have courage to find life and to keep pursuing happiness. Some say they wish they had taken opportunities when they had had the chance, and now they are encouraged to grasp life in a new and positive way. I am open. I always have been. Life is to be shared. Experiences to be mentioned. Mistakes to be named. Happiness to be talked about. I am a passionate person. I feel deeply. I am all about the words. I am a writer. A conveyor of thoughts and emotions. I am an encourager interested in the lives and thoughts of others. I am a lover of life. I have found myself lately on a path with ruts and bumps, but because of my absolute belief in the future, I have learned to navigate the obstacles and still have hope in things to come.

It helps to have a positive person by your side. This one has a beautiful heart, in-spite of many disappointments in life. I have learned from him about forgiveness, about placing your absolute trust in God's will, and about patience. To touch another life and make an impact is the ultimate satisfaction in this life. To influence someone in a worthy way, with love and compassion, and just to mean something. I will continue with the words when I feel them. Words are power. Words can bruise. Words can enlighten. They can lift. They can connect with another, maybe one who needs to know that they have hope and a future. Hope looks forward. Speak words of hope. Think thoughts of the future and things that are still to come.

I wanted it all to be perfect. But then, what was perfect? I learned "perfect" had to change, and so did I.

Two years into being a widow, my brother introduced me to a man who was his neighbor. We had lived in the same town in the past, attended the same high school, and had some of the same friends, yet we had never met before. There was an instant connection for me, and he says for him too. There was a gentleness to his manner and a positiveness in the way he carried himself and in his smile. He was alone. About two months after we met, we had our first date. We went to visit his ninety-three-year-old mother at a rehab facility and took her out to eat. We joked about how rarely you meet the parents on the first date. When he brought me home, we talked, and there seemed to be an ease and comfortableness that we both felt. We decided that although we were separated by about one hundred miles, we wanted to pursue this and see where it went. It went well, and after a year of dating and commuting to see each other on the weekends, we decided to take a chance and make a commitment to each other.

The following writings are my feelings at the time of this rebirth and renewing of my life. I continue to strive for happiness and to keep a feeling of contentment and joy for life. Not every day is easy, and second-chance relationships are not always problem free, but our hearts are genuine, and our commitment is solid. We both feel that the Lord led us to one another, and it is our love for Him and each other that keep us looking ahead.

When the dawn broke, my mind was still on the woods and the water. It was a short time before the hustle and bustle of a million lives would be converging on a myriad of highways and byways where I live. And the noise and the worries of the world would be carried around all day in a countless number of vehicles and voices. I wanted my heart to be still. I wanted my ears only filled with the sweet sound of the birds and the wind in the tall branches of the pine trees I had just left. I wanted my eyes only to see the beauty of the early-morning sunrise dancing across the waters of that lake. I wanted my heart to be beating for a purpose and a reason to rejoice in this life. So, when the dawn broke, my mind was still on the woods and the water—and him.

Chances are best taken when the heart does the leading. Be breathless! Be excited! Be alive!

Yet I still wander where I am headed. Where am I going? I do like this spot I have landed on. It is comfortable and good. I realize that one is never too old to believe, to hope, or to experience something different. Yet the world and life are so very painful at times and want to keep you standing still or moving backward. The old will stick like superglue bonding, and the new is trod upon lightly as not to make a misstep or an error. How do you survive? You must put on wings of freedom and reckless abandon. You must float, never thinking too deeply but only grabbing hold of life that lies before you. You must believe in living, newness, and change when it is apparent that those are what lie ahead. Glance over your shoulder, but do not gaze too long into the past, for you will lose your courage, meaning, and destiny.

I had been looking backward, he had been looking forward, and somehow our paths crossed. He taught me about believing, letting go, forgiveness, and adventure. I taught him about unconditional love, loyalty, and trust. We decided to head in the same direction together. In sunshine and in shadow, we would be there for each other. And in the moonlight, under the stars, we vowed to travel one path together forever.

Sometimes we are restless and think one place would be better than another. Then when we reach the other, our heart longs for where we were before. But when we find that person who makes us feel whole, the contentment and the feeling of home become that person. Then there is no anxiousness to roam or longing for anything before. It is a beautiful thing to have a home.

He took me to the middle of the lake, where there were no problems or disappointments and no hurts or worries. We drifted a while and talked of beautiful things and happiness and dreams. The sun, low in the west, seemed to hesitate to meet the horizon. Its rays of muted light occasionally peeked from behind the clouds as we drifted. There was no other soul upon those waters that evening, but if there had been, we would not have noticed. We were lost in thoughts of beautiful things, and happiness and dreams, as we drifted on glassy waters in the middle of the lake.

To truly be loved and know it, and to feel secure in that love, is the greatest gift upon this earth. It fills the heart and all the senses with abounding passion and complete satisfaction.

Love is many things.

If you have it, it surrounds you

With blankets of security, loyalty, respect, peace, contentment, completeness.

There will be no doubts.

There will be no other.

It can be identified with just a look or a touch,

But it can die

Without nurturing or tending to very gently.

Or without words or actions.

Without the glances or the touches.

So strong, yet so fragile.

It was the way he made me feel without saying a word. He caressed my battered spirit with the touch of his hand. His want of me was apparent by the tenderness of his gaze. His gentle manner was like a low-burning fire: warm, comfortable, and safe. I knew he had been wounded too, and perhaps the pain he had been dealt softened him, molded him into the perfect loving rescuer of my heart.

The depth of love is measured by the width of the void that is present when hearts are separated. When the heart hurts, the mind cannot be satisfied. Then you have your answer to the question "Is it love?" The heart wants what it wants and is unyielding to any other pleasure. And the mind reasons all thoughts on the matter and rests its decision with the heart's desire.

I wanted blue skies and summer days forever. I have had more than enough dark and sunless hours. My life went spinning out of control without warning. But now, I have been learning to adjust to my feet on some steady ground and some strength. I am adjusting to someone who can sweep away any storm cloud headed my way with just his smile, his voice, and his touch. My life was spinning out of control again, but in an exquisitely sublime way.

It was easy between the two of them. Mainly because they both knew what they wanted. It was each other.

I saw the open gate by the moonlight's glow, and I knew

This was the right place, the right place to go.

I had felt the warmth from the one whose heart was inside,

And I knew this was where, where I must reside,

For his heart was as open as that garden gate.

And for his love I would not, would not have to wait,

So, through the open gate I did go,

And I found the one, the one who loves me so.

There was an instant connection between their spirits. An unexplained closeness when they were together. They found in each other all that had been missing for so very long.

The wind was blowing, the leaves were turning, and everything was changing, including me. But the difference was I was becoming alive as all of nature was beginning its seasonal expiration. The cool wind felt good upon my cheeks, and the colorful foliage seemed like a beautiful shroud to me. I was wrapping up all my sorrow and casting it to that wind, in that rainbow shroud. I felt messages from God above. There had been unmistakable signs. Who can know for certainty the hand of God? I believed the answer to be in my heart, the center of truth. My heart told me it was true. It was time. Time had not been my friend for years. But now, time had brought me something good, kind, and genuine. Something I needed. I was letting go to the fall wind those sorrowful thoughts and dismal days. My heavenly caretaker was providing me with the one I needed to finish my journey with, to run the race, and he was good, kind, and genuine. Someone I needed. And I was ready.

Choosing to be happy is the best decision you will make. The more you choose it, the more permanent it becomes. I love happy, positive beings, even when things are not easy or right. They maintain an attitude of optimism and the best always. How fortunate to be close to and learn from one whose attitude is full of light and hope. I have had that twice in my life now. I am learning to look for the sunshine in my days. Lucky, blessed, and happy am I, believing also that the light in the moonbeams has power that strengthens me and is making me whole.

He asked, "Would you take a chance, a chance on me?"

And I said, "It might be worth it—worth it to me."

He wasn't really looking, but he had prayed—prayed for someone special to care.

I wasn't really looking but needed someone—someone special to share

The rest of life, the rest of dreams, someone worthy of my heart.

He wasn't afraid, and he would not disappoint; he was the one to fill that part.

His prayers were answered, and my needs were met.

We both knew second chances in this life, you rarely get.

We found something special, so special in each other.

And we knew, no need, no need to search any further.

When I love, it is at full speed. I know no other way but straight ahead with every bit of my heart. I risk it all if I love you. If I decide that you are the one, then I value your heart as much as mine. I treat it tenderly, loving it passionately. Protecting it from hurt at all costs. I will always be true. Steady and constant as the sun and the moon and the stars.

Losing Steve was the toughest loss ever for all of us. I am just thankful for his life, his love, and what I learned from him. I feel his presence often, in birds, in pennies I spy randomly strewn in parking lots, and in floating feathers from above. I am thankful for life before, life after, and life now. I am with a man now who honors him, even though he never met him, and he loves me and values my past. The qualities of both men are rare in this world. I am fortunate beyond words.

His gentleness made me comfortable. His honesty made me secure. His love healed me.

Sometimes it works out, but sometimes it works out beautifully. Sometimes it works out early on, and sometimes it works out much later, when you thought all hope was gone. Sometimes the pieces of life fit together perfectly, although they hadn't in a while. Now their sharp edges have been smoothed by life's hard experiences, and another's life adds the missing pieces you needed to finish your beautiful life puzzle. Hope, faith, and real love complete what you were praying for, and it is not a puzzle anymore but a beautiful picture that you cannot stop looking at.

I am turning the page in my life book. I have not enjoyed all the twists and turns in the previous chapters, but I know the Author has planned this story line, and I am anxious to begin the middle of my "book." Love, joy, and memories linger as I reread my beginning. God whispers to me lately, "There is more." Faith and hope in my favorite Author spur me on to write the next chapters and give me encouragement to be excited with the turning of the pages. I trust His story line, beginning to end, and I know the heavenly epilogue already written. I am extremely blessed.

Time had always been my enemy. Either not enough or too much. It had ruled my life for way too long. I endured the fleeting last days of someone I had loved, and then after the end, time had dragged on and on. I had spent many days trying to adjust to a different life. Trying to find out who I was, all by myself. It was lonely, scary, and confusing. I had to decide whether to live or just exist. My mind and spirit were at odds with each other. My mind suppressed thoughts of change, but my spirit wanted freedom, and my soul desired happiness. In time, God's time, someone entered ever so quietly and gently. His spirit had the perfect message for my heart. His kindness softened the murmuring in my head. His smile and his touch were healing for my soul. He had come just in the nick of time for me. He made time stand still for me. He was just what I needed.

The worthy will show up at the right time,

No lights or whistles or chimes,

And you won't need a sign.

Kindred souls will always find

Another related heart,

And a new beginning will have its start.

It might be seen through their eyes.

It will be soft and gentle and warm,

A tender rescue and a shelter from your storm.

Every person needs just that one,

Though some think they are better with none.

But this girl knows without a doubt

Kindred spirits roam and wander all about,

Always searching, sometimes unaware

For that being, that parallel spirit so rare

That will bring joy and fullness to living,

Not a selfish heart, no taking only giving.

Twists and turns our lives do take,

With happenings and chances that we make.

Re-dos, fixes, and clean slates

God gives to all to change our fate.

So, this I know and believe with all my heart.

This wisdom to all searching souls, I impart.

The worthy will show up at the right time.

No lights or whistles or chimes.

And you won't need a sign.

Kindred hearts will always find

Another related here,

And a new beginning will have its start.

We drifted in the boat on the lake amid the wakes and waves. There was music softly playing on the radio. Our hearts were open, and our conversations were honest. We talked of real life and those things we both had experienced long before. We spoke of things past and present and of hopes of the future. You may speak of Aphrodite, Eros, Cupid, Juno, and Parvati on the subject of love, but I, the deeply romantic thinker, and he, the sensitive realist who drifted upon the lake amid the wakes and waves, know *far more* regarding the subject of love.

It was good to be wanted. It was good to be needed. It was good to be loved. It changed everything.

I had had many disappointments lately in life, but he was not one of them. Little did he know that his honesty had revived me and saved me. His gentleness had soothed my hurts and healed my broken spirit. He cared with no reservations. Loving him was easy.

The old dirt road shined like a satin ribbon under the moon's golden glow. I was traveling in a new direction now. It was away from the city's lights and noise and problems and pain. I could see the heavens with a myriad of twinkling stars blinking on what looked like an endless black carpet. *Peace,* I thought. *This is peace. This is just the place I have wanted to be, and now I want to stay forever.*

My heart beat faster as I neared the place I wanted to be. No one understood how much he meant to me, maybe not even him. I felt it with every fiber of my being. He was where I wanted to be. He was my rainbow after the storm. He was my home.

There once was a girl named Sandra. She was so grateful for a blessed life, so rich and full. A life complete with great children and grandchildren, and the greatest of friends, new and old. And she knew the Lord, and He filled her heart with such happiness that her eyes brimmed with tears several times a day. She thanked Him. How can it be that one like her has been so lucky? She knew deep in her heart that luck had nothing to do with it. Love had everything to do with it. And so, her eyes brimmed with tears again and she thanked the One who loves her so and has taken the time to be with her every single day as she makes her way through this thing called life. There once was a girl named Sandra, and she was grateful for a blessed life, so rich and full.

> Peace I leave with you; my peace I give you. I do not give to you as the world gives. Do not let your hearts be troubled and do not be afraid. (John 14:27 NIV)

I have peace of mind and heart, and I owe it all to my Savior, Jesus Christ. He has led me all my life, but ever so closely since 2010. Through earth-shattering news, through difficult, uncertain years of emotional upheaval, through loss and grieving, through self-doubts, mistakes, and rebuilding myself, and through changes and chances for new happiness. He led me to the perfect person He chose for me to finish my life with, and as I view this beautiful home I have found, I hear Him whisper through the breezes in the trees, "Peace I leave with you; My peace I give you."

I made my way to the big rock that overlooks the cool waters of the lake. The sunlight glistened upon the smooth, blue reservoir, flashing now and then like some heavenly radiant shower, bouncing from ripple to gentle ripple. My thoughts skipped from here to there, and from past to present. I was beginning to feel the ease of normalcy again. The mundaneness, the routine, that at one time I had been bored with, but that was before the storm. The storm changed everything. It changed everyone, but most of all me. There would never be any understanding for some, and even at times to me. I had focused on the moon after the storm. It had a meaning, private thoughts to me that are tender. The moon had saved me many a night when I was lost, confused, hurting, and sometimes angry. It was on those nights that I had walked in the shadows of the evening, bathed in the misty moonlight. It had covered me like a healing balm, and as the darkness moved forward into the morning daylight, so did I. Then there was the rainbow. Colors as vibrant as neon lights. I gazed upon the rainbow that had followed the storm and crossed the blissful skies to meet my moon. Its message was clear to me. My storm had ended. I was content at this moment as I neared my trek to the big rock that overlooked the cool waters of the lake. I had normalcy, routine, and mundaneness again. It felt right. I had had my storm. I would always have my moon, and now I had my redeeming rainbow.

EPILOGUE

My life has changed. I am not as I was, but I know that through my love for Steve and what we shared together for all the years we had, and most especially the last five years, I am better, wiser, and deeper. He was my heart and soul. When you must redesign yourself, the only Architect that I want and recommend is the Lord Jesus Christ. He is faithful, and in His time, He put me back together again and sent me on a new path.

I have found happiness with myself, and in the healing, I have found happiness with a new partner to finish out this life with. He is remarkable in that he encourages me to speak of my past and Steve as often as I need to. We share a genuine love for our families, our friends, our country, our military, and our God.

My children and grandchildren are healing. To have had such a wonderful, loving dad, it is very hard for them to be without him, but they are finding their own way through grief. One thing that binds us is our love for each other and for Steve.

All of life is about changes—some unwanted, some painful, and some a blessing. We are not here to understand it; we are here just to live it.